"Most of us go through a period of life that can be defined as 'living in the *meanwhile*' as we experience disappointment, discouragement, loneliness, rejection, hardship, or suffering. Our situation feels like God isn't answering our prayers. *Meanwhile* explores deep biblical truth while providing poignant application questions that help us to apply Joseph's story to our story and, in turn, point us to God's story. This is a life-changing study."

—Carol Kent,
speaker, author, founder of Speak Up Ministries

"Masterful Bible teacher Carol McLeod helps us find hope when circumstances don't make sense. For everyone wondering when and how God is going to show up and what to do in the waiting, *Meanwhile* reminds you that your God has not left you and He is most assuredly at work in your life."

—Erica Wiggenhorn,
international speaker, author of *An Unexpected Revival*

"Carol McLeod, has done it again! What a masterpiece she has given us in *Meanwhile*! In our world of uncertainty, pull out your Bible and join Carol as she unlocks profound life lessons in this timely study!"

—Becky Harling,
conference speaker, best-selling author of *The Extraordinary Power of Praise*

"*Meanwhile*. The word holds both the lament of longing, and the palpable hope of promise. Joseph knew both—and we do too. In Joseph, we find the courage to live expectantly in God's timing and confidently in God's goodness."

—Angela Donadio,
author, speaker, host of the *Make Life Matter* podcast

"If you think you know all about the Old Testament's Joseph, then I'm delighted to share that there is more to his story! Perhaps your life, like Joseph's, sometimes seems like a roller-coaster full of ups and downs—with plenty of uncertain in-betweens. This weekly study helps the reader learn how to maneuver with grit, grace, gratitude, and glory as we encounter challenge after challenge. This book will help you get to know Joseph and others' stories of trusting the God who walks with us in the waiting."

—Lucinda Secrest McDowell,
award-winning author of *Soul Strong* and *Life-Giving Choices*

"Wow! Carol did a wonderful job of bringing Joseph to life. She also reminded me that the God who worked behind the scenes of Joseph's life is the same God who will meet us in the mundane and the miraculous of our lives too. Everyone who works through this study will come away with hope, encouragement, and an understanding of what can happen in the 'meanwhile' when keeping their eyes fixed on Jesus."

—Jessie Seneca,
author, speaker, founder of More of Him Ministries

"Joseph has always been my favorite biblical character because both my father and I have been in a pit that God has used to transform our lives. My dad's 'meanwhile' was Watergate and mine was my cancer journey. Carol allows us to experience Joseph's pains and his triumphs through a deeper dive of God's Word. Her modern-day examples assure all of us that God also has a plan for us when we face tragedies in our 'meanwhile.'"

—Ginny Dent Brant,
counselor, speaker, author of *Finding True Freedom* and *Unleash Your God-Given Healing*

"I have read many of Carol McLeod's writings and consider *Meanwhile* to be her best. I have known some of the spiritual giants of our generation; few have the depth of revelation from God's Word as Carol; even fewer have overcome such monumental obstacles. Anyone privileged to know Carol senses the presence of Jesus in her life. You will experience the Holy Spirit as you do this new study—*Meanwhile*—and you will be changed."

—Tim Cameron,
author of *The 40-Day Word Fast* and *The 40-Day Word Fast for Couples*

"Carol McLeod doesn't just teach with her words, but she disciples us toward greater intimacy with our God. *Meanwhile* is rooted in biblical truth as we uncover the life of Joseph and leads us into deeper discovery through the twists and turns of circumstance. For every person who's wondering in the waiting and is ready to walk with God regardless, this is the Bible study for you."

—Jenny Randle,
author of *Dream Come True*, minister with Freedom Creatives

"Reading Carol's new book made me recall the TV commercial where the elderly woman falls and screams, 'I've fallen, and I can't get up!' How often do we feel that way when life clobbers us? Carol's Bible study will empower you to grab God's lifeline scriptures, promises, and hope that will fortify your life and bring enduring strength when life's storms hit. God is with us in every *Meanwhile* in life, and this book is the instruction manual."

—Kathleen Cooke,
cofounder of Cooke Media Group, author of *Hope 4 Today*

"Thought provoking. Soul stirring. *Meanwhile* provides encouragement for those of us who are hanging on the cliff of betrayal, rejection, and trauma. *Meanwhile* will meet you at the crossroads of sorrow and suffering and disciple you straight into the destiny God has planned for you. Your flickering hope will burst into a flame once again. It's a must-read for anyone serious about impacting this world for Jesus!"

—Christine A. Christopher,
author of *Until the Day Breaks and the Shadows Flee*

"In this study of the life of Joseph, Carol allows us to enjoy the story in a fresh new way. You will find yourself inspired, refreshed, challenged, and convicted by the Holy Spirit. Carol will expand your understanding and perspective of how God is always working in your 'meanwhiles' weaving His hope and purposes into your life.

—Diane Zarlengo,
senior pastor's wife, director of women's ministry, church prayer coordinator

MEANWHILE

MEETING GOD IN THE WAIT

Carol McLeod

Birmingham, Alabama

Meanwhile

Iron Stream
An imprint of Iron Stream Media
100 Missionary Ridge
Birmingham, AL 35242
IronStreamMedia.com

Cover design by Melinda Martin
ISBN: 978-1-56309-556-6 (paperback)
ISBN: 978-1-56309-557-3 (e-book)
1 2 3 4 5—26 25 24 23 22

Lovingly dedicated to my second-born son,

Christopher Burton McLeod.

You have known the "meanwhile" days in life, haven't you?

And yet you carry on . . . loving your children, pursuing your passions, and being a purveyor of goodness and kindness wherever you go.

I pray that you will continue to have a heart like that of Joseph and be aware of the Lord's presence in the middle of your circumstances.

He is with you, dear Christopher, just as He was with Joseph.

I am proud of you and the man you have become. You are always, always in my heart.

"We were made for resurrection and someday we're going to get back home. But right now, we're living in the meantime."

CONTENTS

ACKNOWLEDGMENTS

I'll admit it . . . whenever I pick up a new book, after I read the dedication, I always turn to the acknowledgments. I always hope to see who the author has honored in her chapter of gratitude. I long to see who her friends are, what words she uses to describe her family, and what accolades she gives to those who have come alongside to help in the process.

You see, writing is a process; it is a long and arduous journey and no man or woman dare tread the pathway of writing without the refreshment of family, the friends who help carry the luggage, and the always sweaty service of coworkers.

These people are my "background vocalists" in the truest sense of the calling. They sing enthusiastically and on-pitch day after day after long day, never asking for the spotlight.

From the bottom of my heart, thank you.

Thank you, **Craig**, for choosing me, for serving the Lord wholeheartedly, and for so much kindness that I never have felt I deserved. Thank you for being a shepherd, a coach, and now a friend to our children. I am deeply grateful for you.

Thank you, **Matthew**, for forgiving me for all my first-time mama mistakes and for loving me still. Your strength, wisdom, and excellence never cease to amaze me. You are my son and my friend. You are always in my heart. I am profoundly thankful for you.

Thank you, **Christopher,** for the gift of song that you have always provided for our family. You are truly the kindest person that I know. Whether you live near or far, you are always in my heart. I am infinitely grateful for you.

Thank you, **Jordan**, for your prayers, for your support, and for your cheerfulness. I don't just love you . . . but I also like you! You are our miracle child and you were born to serve God at this moment in history! Live for Him always. You are always in my heart! I am beyond thankful for you.

Thank you, **Joy**, for always living up to your name and for lavishing the delight that is uniquely yours on everyone that you meet. You are my daughter and my friend. I am so proud of you, especially now. Your call to ministry and to motherhood is obvious. I am honored to be your mom.

Thank you, **Joni,** for the years of sweet camaraderie that we shared as you were growing up. Those were some of the very favorite days of my entire life. Know that I am your mom—and nothing will ever change that! You are loved completely. You are always in my heart. I am so thankful for you.

Thank you, **Emily,** for the vitality and strength you have brought to our family after marrying Matthew, the first-born son. How brave you were to enter this family filled with opinions, creativity, and strong wills! You have been a delight to us all and I am grateful that you are my daughter-in-love.

Thank you, **Allie,** for choosing Jordan and for loving us all unconditionally. Your prayers have already moved mountains and your heart for worship is pure and brave. Know that I am grateful – beyond grateful – to call you my daughter-in-love and my friend!

And then, to **Olivia, Ian, Wesley, Amelia, Boyce, Elizabeth Joy, Jack, Haven, and Isla Ruth**. You are the ones who will carry the torch of family and faith to the next generation. Learn well, listen intently, watch carefully, and obey willingly. God has greatness hidden inside each one of you! And always remember that it pays to serve Jesus.

Thank you, **Mom and Leo**, for your prayers, your faith, and your encouragement. I ache to be with you but I know that the Lord is faithful in His care of you. I will always be "your girl."

Thank you, **Nanny,** for your example of godly living and persistent prayer!

Thank you to my dad, **Norman Burton,** who has escaped time and now lives in eternity. I wouldn't be the woman I am today without your leadership and example. All the credit goes to you and all the glory goes to God!

Thank you to my dear friend and coworker, **Angela Storm.** You are a gift to me and to this ministry. Thank you for your labor of love, for your attention to details, for your prayer support, and for your faith. I love serving God with you!

Thank you to my friend and fellow warrior, **Christy Christopher**. You are making a difference, Christy. Never doubt the assignment on your life or the power that you have been given! I love "making hell smaller and heaven bigger" with you!

Thank you to **Keri Spring** whose dedicated service to Carol McLeod Ministries has helped us to soar. You, my friend, are simply amazing! What did we ever do without Keri?!

Thank you to the entire staff of **Carol McLeod Ministries**: Angela Storm, Susan Meyers, Linda Zielinski, Keri Spring, Caleb Wiley, Kim Worden, and Christy Christopher. It is an undeserved honor to work with all of you as we endeavor to take the joy of His presence to this generation. You are appreciated, loved, and prayed for daily.

I must give a deep and sincere thank-you to the **Carol McLeod Ministries Board of Directors**: Angela Storm, Kim Pickard Dudley, Sue Hilchey, Shannon Maitre, Tim Harner, Taci Darnelle, and Suzanne Kuhn. You all are the foundation of everything that we do—thanks for being rock solid! Your wisdom, expertise, and personal support are invaluable.

It is my deep honor to give a rich and heartfelt thank-you to the entire staff at **Iron Stream Media**, especially to John Herring, Bradley Isbell, and Suzanne Kuhn. *Meanwhile* is a miraculous answer to prayers that I have prayed for decades. Thank you for believing in the message of my heart and my commitment to truth.

Thank you, **Johnnie Hampton,** for dreaming with me and for believing in the message of this ministry. Your professional and personal support means the world to me.

Thank you, **Chris Busch**, for your quiet and steady guidance. Your friendship is a true gift.

Warrior Moms—What an honor it has been to fight battles with you! We are standing in strong faith that with God nothing is impossible. Thank you for holding up my arms in the battle.

Thank you also to the group of women who answer the desperate e-mails that come into **Carol McLeod Ministries**: Debby Summers, Angela Storm, Carolyn Hogan, Diane Phelps, Jill Janus, Shannon Maitre, Susie Hilchey, Keri Spring, Beth Nash, Debby Edwards, Linda Zielinski, Suzanne Adorian, Brenda Mutton, Kim Worden, Laurie Rudolph, Taci Darnell, Elaine Wheatley, Katie Martin, Deb Cook, Joanne Crain, and Christy Christopher—God is using you in mighty and dramatic ways! I am honored to partner with you in prayer and in encouragement.

And then, to a magnificent team of friends who fill my life with encouragement and joy. Each one of you has helped me get through too many "meanwhiles" to count!

Carolyn Hogan
Lisa Keller
Jill Janus
Dawn Frink
Debby Edwards
Diane Phelps
Brenda Mutton
Elaine Wheatley
Becky Harling
Melissa Thompson
Marilynda Lynch
Joy Knox
Sue Hilchey
Kim Pickard Dudley
Shannon Maitre
Christy Christopher

And to **Jesus, my Lord and Savior**! Thank You for calling me, equipping me, anointing me, and choosing me for Your grand purposes. I live to make hell smaller and heaven bigger! I live to honor You with every breath, with every word, and with every minute of my life! Thank You, Father, for allowing me to teach the eternal truth that is found only in the Word of God. All of the joy that I need is found in You!

My heart overflows with a good theme;
I address my verses to the King;
My tongue is the pen of a ready writer.

—Psalm 45:1

INTRODUCTION

There are many stories in the Bible that contain the eternal power to deeply touch a tender part in each one of us—I believe the story of Joseph is such a story. I for one have long been fascinated by this coddled young man who was bullied by his brothers, sold into slavery, sexually harassed by an older woman, yet became the second most powerful man in the ancient world. It seems like a ridiculous movie plot, doesn't it?

I must tell you at the onset of this study that Joseph has always been my favorite Old Testament character. While others might choose Ruth, Esther, Moses, or David—for me it has always been Joseph. One of the reasons I relate so deeply to his story is that he possessed the tenacity and resolve to serve God in the most critical and ferocious of times. Oh, how I long for the tenacity and resolve of this young man who lived thousands of years ago.

In days of devastation and loss, I often asked myself the question, *I wonder what Joseph would do if he were dealing with this trauma?*

I am convinced that as we study the story of Joseph together, you will realize a startling truth as I have. The God who worked behind the scenes in Joseph's life is the same God who is able to do a mighty work on your behalf. When we allow God's involvement in the writing of our stories, He can turn all our "meanwhiles" into miracles.

Joseph experienced a "meanwhile" that included a pit, slavery, and prison. Your meanwhile will certainly look circumstantially different from Joseph's ancient story; however, living through a "meanwhile" is common to the human experience. I simply define a "meanwhile" as the test of faith between a crisis and God's *visible* intervention.

Our loving and omnipotent Father can revolutionize the most devastating moment of your life. He can transform it into your finest hour—just as He did for Joseph.

The Holy Spirit, Joseph, and You

The circumstances of Joseph's life seem almost too contrived and improbable for a true story. But factually true they are. The events of Joseph's life are verifiably genuine and undeniably astonishing. The reason I know this is because they have been recounted on the sacred pages of the Bible, which is our source for all truth.

The Holy Spirit, the finest Teacher in all eternity past, and all eternity yet to come, knew you and I would need to extract timeless truth from the story of Joseph. This is why the Bible states the following:

> *For whatever was written in former days was written for our*
> *instruction, that through endurance and through the*
> *encouragement of the Scriptures we might have hope.*
>
> —*Romans 15:4 ESV*

The Holy Spirit, who is a genius at everything, recorded the story of Joseph in the Bible through the hand of Moses. This is the same man who transcribed the Ten Commandments and the leader who delivered the children of Israel out of Egypt. The Holy Spirit determined that you and I, living in the first part of the twenty-first century, needed the story of Joseph in order to develop endurance, for encouragement in our faith, and to live a life of hope. I believe all of that and even more will take place as you study Joseph's life unfolding in the book of Genesis.

I have often wondered, perhaps a bit presumptuously, if the Holy Spirit were to write about my life in the Bible, what details He would include. Would the Holy Spirit share the escapades of my teenage years? Would He have the audacity to recount the details of my romance with a wonderful man of God—now my husband? Would the Holy Spirit skillfully tell of my anguish as I wandered through depression for nearly a decade? Would He describe my fierce battle with infertility? Would the Holy Spirit think it important to depict for all of God's people, in all of the epochs yet to come, about the early morning hours when as just a little girl, I read the Bible with my dad? Perhaps, the Holy Spirit would recite the powerful moment when I first heard God's voice, or the passionate Sunday evenings I spent at the altar as a child.

I must admit it's sobering to ponder what particulars the Holy Spirit might deem impressive or important enough to transcribe for the entire world to see. I imagine any of us might feel curiosity at the thought. But we can be assured of this—the Holy Spirit included every necessary detail of Joseph's life for us to be instructed in truth, in perseverance, in encouragement, and in hope.

Partnering with the Word

As you read the story of Joseph with me, you will have the opportunity to answer daily questions within the scope of our study. I have prayerfully considered how to involve you while bringing comfort to your "meanwhile." My heart's desire in writing this Bible study is that it would strengthen your walk with the Lord and propel you into your destiny in Christ. Only the Bible can do that.

I hope you will take the time to carefully answer each question. I have found applying the principles in the Word of God to my personal life provides revelation knowledge, springing to vibrant meaning inside of me. Answering the questions and becoming part of the Joseph conversation might feel challenging to you at first, but believe me when I assure you that God wants to know your heart. He is interested in your responses and thoughts. As you participate, you just may hear Him whisper, responding to you as He helps you persevere, delivering hope to your weary heart.

At the end of each day's work, you will find a quote to ponder, as a gift to you. I believe as we choose to reflect on the thoughts of great men and women who have gone before us, we ourselves will begin to think greater thoughts.

Hidden Treasure

Each week, I will also urge you to commit a Bible verse to memory. I have titled this part of the assignment, *Hidden Treasure*. When we hide God's Word in our hearts, joy increases vibrantly and wisdom flows unabated. Who wouldn't want that?

I know so many adult women who no longer memorize the Word of God as part of their spiritual disciplines. I must tell you, these women are missing out on peace, strength, and divine insight. Let's become a generation of women who treasure the Word of God in our hearts and in our minds.

How blessed are those who observe His testimonies,
Who seek Him with all their heart.

—Psalm 119:2

The Joseph Lifestyle

After each week's daily reading, I have also added a component unique to this Bible study. Though this added portion is certainly optional, I believe it will prove to be one of your favorite parts of the entire study. At the end of each "Day 5" and prior to the beginning of the following week, you will find a story of a woman who lived wholeheartedly for God during days of great pain—just as Joseph did. Some of these women might be familiar to you, while you may not have heard the stories of others. I believe as we examine people from history who dared to live with honor, integrity, and a heart of worship, even when life was cruel, that we, too, will be inspired. We discover the resolve and intention to live for Christ during our difficult days as we are cheered on by their heroic narratives.

Here We Go

So . . . put on your sandals, bring a box of tissue, and prepare to go on the greatest adventure of your life. Let's travel through time and see the fingerprint of the Father on the life of Joseph.

There is no indication that God explained to Joseph what He was doing through those many years of heartache or how the pieces would eventually fit together. He had no way of knowing that he would eventually enjoy a triumphal reunion with his family. He was expected, as you and I are, to live out his life one day at a time in something less than complete understanding. What pleased God was Joseph's faithfulness when nothing made sense.

—James C. Dobson
Life on the Edge

Week 1

Where Does Your Story Begin?

Day 1

"A Mighty Mean-while"

We have all experienced a "meanwhile" in life when faced with frustration and the unique pain that endless waiting stirs up. During my meanwhiles, I often wondered where God was and if He was even aware of what I was going through. However, I can assure you that for every meanwhile you encounter, there is also a God strategically laboring behind the scenes in your circumstances. He's working all things together for His good, your good, and for His glory.

I have learned that often a meanwhile can produce a mighty long and incredibly challenging *mean-while*. In this type of season, a meanwhile feels unfairly cruel and unkind. Such is the story of Joseph. The historical account of this young man will convince you that when God is involved, He is more than able to turn all your meanwhiles into miracles. Consider the following three questions:

⏳ *What is the most painful meanwhile experience you have ever faced?*

⏳ *What were some of the practices or disciplines that enabled you to get through your meanwhile?*

⏳ *Why do you think our examination into the life of Joseph from the Old Testament is titled Meanwhile?*

Your Favorite

Meanwhile is an in-depth Bible study covering the history of Joseph, found in Genesis chapter 37 and then in chapters 39–50. The importance of researching the people, customs, challenges, and victories of Old Testament events establishes a valuable foundation for our walk in Jesus Christ. The Old Testament presents dynamic truths that will enable you to live wholeheartedly today for Christ and for His kingdom. This makes me wonder . . .

⧗   *Who is your favorite Old Testament character?*

⧗   *What lesson(s) did you learn from this person's story?*

A Victim and Yet a Victor

If we were only to consider Joseph's story from a circumstantial viewpoint rather than from a biblical perspective, we would certainly identify him as a victim. Horrific circumstances, family dysfunction, undeserved slavery, unfair accusations, and sexual harassment is the stuff of Joseph's life. However, none of those adverse and extreme conditions impacted the ability of Joseph to walk in his God-ordained destiny. The sordid pain that enveloped Joseph's young life eventually propelled him into his purpose.

My friend, you are the "Joseph" of your own story. There are situations, relationships, abuses, and rejections that might try to victimize you and the person you were created to be. However, never forget there is a God working faithfully to transform what the enemy meant for evil into something beautiful and purposeful.

No matter what you have gone through in life and regardless of how Satan has attacked your family, your productivity, or your freedom, know that God is big and powerful enough to right the wrong. He will set you free to glorify Himself in you.

⧗   *What has given you hope when you experienced circumstantial or relational pain?*
Be specific.

Hidden Treasure: Read this verse out loud several times today and write it out on a 3x5 card. Think about this verse throughout the week and begin to commit it to memory:

For whatever was written in former days was written for our instruction, that through endurance and through the encouragement of the Scriptures we might have hope.

—Romans 15:4 ESV

You can't go back and change the beginning, but you can start where you are and change the ending.

—James Sherman
Rejection

Day 2

Let's Start at the Very Beginning

Rather than commencing with Joseph's riveting story, let's instead start at *your* beginning. After we examine the foundational issues of your life, we will leap back through millennia to uncover the fascinating details of Joseph's tale. For many, our stories began before we were even conceived.

I was born in a nondescript town on a country road in the middle of the twentieth century. I attended a one-room schoolhouse in the town where my dad owned the general store, taught Sunday school, and cultivated a one-acre garden plot every year. No one of any consequence took note of my birth, but I was loved, wanted, and cared for in the most tender of ways. My beginning might seem unpretentious to you, but to me, it was rich and wonderful. What about your start?

⏳ *Describe the foundational years of your life with adjectives rather than with sentences. Perhaps choose 3–5 adjectives that give an appropriate description of your childhood years:*

1. _____

2. _____

3. _____

4. _____

5. _____

I have a decorative pillow placed lovingly on the bed in our guest bedroom. In lovely blue script it reads, *Home is where your story begins.* Your childhood environment, the atmosphere of your home, and the people who lived in that place with you all contributed to the foundational issues of your life.

Perhaps your personal story started with an unplanned pregnancy. If that is the case, you might believe your life can be summed up with the lonely word "unwanted."

Maybe you were born into a family with an alcoholic father or an emotionally removed mother. Likely, your formative years were marked by yelling, screaming, blame, and abuse. If this describes the opening chapter of your life, you probably believe you are incapable of making anyone happy. You might also hold as your cornerstone the feeling of being unloved or not being enough.

Maybe you were a girl when your father made it very clear that he had always wanted a boy. If this parental disappointment set the stage of your life, you have surely wandered around in the murky fog of lost identity.

I hope you were loved unconditionally from the first moment your mother held you in her arms while tears ran unhindered down her young cheeks. I hope you were raised in a household of faith and can say, with me, that my home life was not perfect, but it was pretty wonderful. Whatever your start, let's take a courageous look at it.

⧖   *What one event in your childhood helped fashion you into the woman you are today?*

⧖   *If you experienced a healthy childhood, what benefits or blessings from that experience strengthen you even now?*

⧖   *If your childhood was difficult, how has God redeemed your pain?*

Nothing Wasted

However complicated the foundational years of your life, know that nothing is wasted by your Creator. He is able to take any abuse, scandal, addiction, or disappointment and miraculously revolutionize it into something wonderful for His kingdom and glory. You were not forgotten—nor were you ever alone.

Reading the following scripture out loud and replacing your name in every place where it says "me," "my," or "I" will instill the truth of who you are. Do this as many times as it takes for you to feel God's inestimable value of you.

For You formed my inward parts;
You wove me in my mother's womb.
I will give thanks to You, for I am fearfully
and wonderfully made;
Wonderful are Your works,
And my soul knows it very well.
My frame was not hidden from You,
When I was made in secret,
And skillfully wrought in the depths of the earth;
Your eyes have seen my unformed substance;
And in Your book were all written
The days that were ordained for me,
when as yet there was not one of them.

—Psalm 139:13–16

⧗ *Create a list of things that make you grateful about your childhood or your young adult years. Don't hold back. Be thorough and mindful of the ways God has blessed you, despite your circumstances.*

⧗ *If the Holy Spirit were to write a chronicle of your life, what events do you believe He would include?*

⧗ *Spend some time thinking about our treasure verse for the week.*

Teach me to treat all that comes to me with peace of soul and with firm conviction that Your will governs all.

—Elisabeth Elliot
A Path Through Suffering

Day 3

Once Upon a Time

The story of Joseph told in Genesis, which you may know, opens the Pentateuch. Pronounced "Pen" + "tuh" + "tyook," it consists of the first five books of the Bible. Traditionally, Moses is credited as the main author of the Pentateuch.

As I study the writings of Moses and dig deeply for eternal treasure among the sacred pages, I can assure you that Genesis is not merely the beginning of the Bible. It is the very foundation of God's Word. The historical accounts revealed in the Book of Genesis set the stage for all that is to come for the people of God. The themes in Genesis lay the infrastructure for everything the Holy Spirit divulges later in subsequent books of the Bible.

Let's Dig In

Joseph's father, Jacob, was a patriarch of the people of God. Jacob was the son of Isaac, who was the son of Abraham. Isaac was only a sojourner in the land but his son, Jacob, Joseph's father, dwelt in the land of Canaan. Canaan was their home, and their roots lodged deeply into this place of settlement.

> *Now Jacob lived in the land where his father had sojourned, in the land of Canaan. These are the records of the generations of Jacob.*
>
> *Joseph, when seventeen years of age, was pasturing the flock with his brothers while he was still a youth, along with the sons of Bilhah and the sons of Zilpah, his father's wives. And Joseph brought back a bad report about them to their father.* **(Genesis 37:1–2)**

Joseph was the eleventh of the twelve sons of Jacob, the first son born to Rachel, who was Jacob's favorite and dearly loved wife. Do you know the names of Joseph's brothers?

⏳ *Make a list of all the sons of Jacob as well as who their mothers were. This will help you keep the family tree straight as we continue our study. You can find this list in Genesis 35:23–26.*

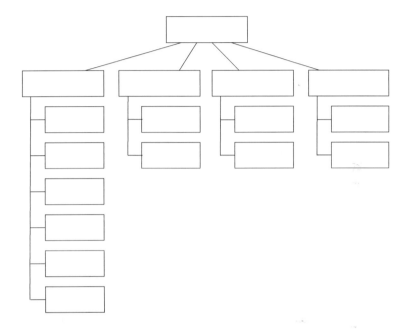

A Leader Leads

Many theologians believe Joseph was in charge of the flock and his brothers, although he was only seventeen years old.[1] As the one in leadership, Joseph was expected and even encouraged to make full reports concerning the behavior and the work ethic of those under his watch. The syntax in this verse actually implies the verbiage, "Joseph was shepherding his brothers."[2]

Joseph's leadership skills were honed even from his boyhood. God trained Joseph in his formative years for what he would be called upon to do in his adult life. Although Joseph was the unlikely overseer of his brothers, this jurisdiction in the family order prepared him for the assignment he would have decades later while in Egypt. Joseph gained expertise as a young man in Canaan, learning to lead in the face of improbable situations and over dubious followers. In Joseph, we meet a rare young man. As we observe his life, no matter what the conditions, we see a striking combination of grace and power. Joseph constantly exhibits amazing self-control and incorruptible purity. Oh, to be like Joseph.

⧗ *List three attributes you believe are vital for leaders to possess, regardless of their age.*

1. _____

2. _____

3. _____

⧗ *Who is the best leader you know? Would you take some time to pray for this person? Also, you might want to consider writing a thank you note to this leader.*

⧗ *Do you consider yourself a leader? Who are you leading?*

Now, for some reason, Joseph brought back a bad report about his brothers to his father. Although the Bible doesn't specify what this bad report was, there is evidence that his brothers were guilty of not keeping the Noahic food laws. "For he had seen them eating flesh torn from a living animal, the ears and the tails."[3]

Joseph, while in the field with his brothers, observed behavior he knew his father would not approve of, so he did what a good leader must always do—he took it to the top. When there is compromise or a poor work ethic among a group of laborers, the boss must always be informed. Joseph simply told the truth to his father. He maintained a commitment to righteous living that was foreign and perhaps even preposterous to his older brothers. How do you evaluate leadership?

⧗ *Do you think Joseph was a tattletale or was he just doing his job?*

⧗ *Do you find confrontation difficult or easy?*

⧖ *What are some godly principles to remember when confronting a difficult situation?*

⧖ *Read Colossians 3:12–17 and journal any words of wisdom applicable to dealing with challenging situations that involve difficult people.*

⧖ *Spend some time today meditating on the treasure verse for the week and make sure you are committing it to memory.*

Down through the years, I turned to the Bible and found
in it all that I needed.

—*Ruth Bell Graham*

Day 4

For Good

Can I make two confessions before we go any further into our study of Joseph? First of all, I am a read-aholic. I read morning, noon, and night. I am addicted to that five-letter word—books. And, in addition to my self-professed book addiction, I have acquired yet another habit. You may not approve of this one.

I always read the last chapter first. It's true. Before I decide whether or not I will read a particular book, I always go to the final chapter at the onset of my excursion into the storyline. I do this because I love a happy ending, and if a book does not conclude victoriously, with good triumphing over evil, I refuse to make time for the convoluted tale. There isn't enough money in the universe to pay me to read a book that ends sloppily, with strings left untied or with questions yet unanswered.

So, perhaps you have surmised our next step in the story of Joseph. Let's skip ahead and read the end of his story. Some of the final verses will remove the suspense of what God was doing through all the difficulties of Joseph's young life. And I hope it will also encourage you. One thing you can trust—God is working behind the scenes for you, just as He was for Joseph.

Now, let's leave the young leader for a moment and fast forward to Joseph's decades-older self, found in the last chapter of Genesis.

> *Then his brothers also came and fell down before him and said, "Behold, we are your servants." But Joseph said to them, "Do not be afraid, for am I in God's place?"*
> *"As for you, you meant evil against me, but God meant it for good in order to bring about this present result to preserve many people alive." (Genesis 50:18–20)*

The passage we will linger upon is this, "You meant evil against me, but God meant it for good." Upon this one phrase from a singular scripture in the Old Testament lies the theology that will change your perspective of life forever.

Remember, Genesis is not only the "beginning" of the Bible, but it is also the "foundation" of God's Word. The truth of this book is so vast and deep that upon it lies a significant portion of our Christian teaching.

No matter what you endure or how high your disappointments pile up, God is at work. When Satan attacks you, God is still on the throne reigning over every event. Ultimately, nothing can prevent Him from creating a masterpiece of greatness in you and through you.

When hard times hit, hold onto that phrase, "You meant evil against me, but God meant it for good." Grip this truth now, and we will soon add another scripture to it, causing the words of Joseph to literally come alive in your life.

Everyone's Favorite

One of everyone's favorite verses is found in the book of Jeremiah. Perhaps you have seen this message on a graduation card, read it daily on a wall plaque in your home, or memorized it to remind yourself of God's plans for your life:

"For I know the plans that I have for you," declares the Lord, "plans for welfare and not for calamity to give you a future and a hope."

—Jeremiah 29:11

The word translated "plans" is from the Hebrew *machashabah*. However, *machashabah* means so much more than mere plans. This ancient, multilayered word can also be translated as "thought," "device," "intention," "purpose," "invention," "imagination," or "artistic work." If you go searching for buried treasure in *machashabah*, you will certainly find it there.

Joseph, as he looked at the wrinkled faces and paunchy bellies of his brothers, decades after they had sold him into slavery, used a term that came from the root word *machashabah*. When he declared, "You **meant** evil against me, but God **meant** it for good," *machashabah* was at play.

God can take anything that anyone does to us, no matter how evil or abusive it might be, and He can "machashab" it for our good. God will never allow anything into our lives that He is not able to "machashab" for a redemptive plan. He can morph the schemes and plans of the enemy into something incredibly wonderful. You serve a God who is well able to "machashab" human pain, disappointment, and mistreatment into something glorious that will "preserve many people alive." This is your destiny, my friend.

⧗ *What has God "machashab'd" for good in your life? I want you to write it out below, but I also want you to look for the opportunity to tell someone else about it this week. The story of Joseph was told to instill us with hope and encouragement, and I believe your story will do the same for someone else.*

You can be assured that the story of Joseph will end victoriously and magnificently. And I can also assure you, as a woman of the twenty-first century, God will cause your story to end victoriously and magnificently.

He Is Working

⏳   *Would you write out Romans 8:28 below?*

⏳   *In Joseph's story, he told his brothers that God worked for good what they had intended for evil. Romans 8:28 declares that God works all things together for good. What is your definition of the word good?*

⏳   *What does Romans 8:28 say is a prerequisite for God to work a situation together for good?*

⏳   *Now Read Romans 8:28–31 out loud. How can you apply these verses to the story of Joseph?*

⏳   *How can you apply these verses to the story of your life?*

⧗ Often, I have realized the "good" God does is not necessarily accomplished by changing my circumstances, but it is accomplished by changing me. How have difficult relationships and circumstances in your life changed you for the good?

⧗ Have you ever been mistreated by someone you loved and trusted? Have you fully forgiven that person? Joseph forgave his brothers to the extent that he could actually declare a blessing over their lives. Perhaps you could write a letter of blessing to the person or people who mistreated you. Whether you send it or not is up to you—sometimes just writing a note of forgiveness and blessing is enough to set you free.

⧗ As always, spend some time memorizing the verse for the week. You will be glad you did.

The Lord gets his best soldiers out of the highlands of affliction.

—Charles Spurgeon
Gleanings Among the Sheaves

Day 5

You Are Joseph

We have barely commenced our study of Joseph but have already solidly laid an interesting and personal foundation. Today, it is time to take out your pens, your notebooks, and your mirrors, as we continue digging for gold in the biblical account of Joseph. You might wonder why you need a mirror, so let me explain.

Whenever I read a great novel, not only do I read the last chapter first, but I also try to imagine who I could be in the grand story I am reading. It won't surprise you to learn I usually want to be the heroine—the girl dressed in gorgeous clothes, and although she has been cruelly mistreated, eventually finds true love. In *The Sound of Music*, I am always Maria. In *Pride and Prejudice*, I am Elizabeth Bennet. And in *Gone with the Wind*, I am definitely NOT the self-centered Scarlett, but instead, the overlooked and sweetly strong Melanie.

In the historical commentary of Joseph, my friend, you are him—you are the hero. You could almost replace your name with his name in every place, in every situation, and in every relationship.

Three Ways

I believe there are three ways to read the Bible. First of all you can read it theologically, which is for the express purpose of learning more about God and His flawless character. When you read the Bible theologically, you are intent on one principal focus. *I must know the God of the Bible.* What a wonderful way to read the Word of God.

The second approach to Bible reading explores it historically. Knowing that every event truly happened, and every person actually lived, bringing it alive. What a vivid and thoughtful way to read the Bible.

And finally, the third method is to absorb it personally. When you read the Bible in a personal manner, you discover that every promise, principle, and lesson was meant for you. If you were the only person in all recorded history to open the sacred pages of the Word of God, the Holy Spirit would still have written it. So, let's consider the following.

⧗   *In what manner do you chiefly read the Bible? Theologically? Historically? Or personally?*

⧗   *Do you believe that one of the three ways is more preferable for studying the Bible? Which way do you read in your daily devotions?*

His Absolute Favorite

When you and I read the verse below in a personal manner and understand that the Holy Spirit desires to teach us a particular lesson, a truth becomes clear. We realize that God the Father has an intimate and favorable relationship with His children. He blesses us beyond understanding.

> **Now Israel loved Joseph more than all his sons, because he was the son of his old age; and he made him a varicolored tunic. (Genesis 37:3)**

It's a challenge to understand the favor of God, isn't it? God doesn't *choose* favorites like a teacher, or a friend might have the bent to do, but you are His favorite. You are His favorite because He created you and He loves you with an everlasting love. His eyes are always on your life, and He is always thinking good thoughts about you. You, my friend, are always on His mind.

⧗   *What do you think it means to be "God's favorite"?*

⧗   *What is your definition of "the favor of God"?*

⧗   *Read Psalm 5:12, Psalm 30:5 and Proverbs 8:35. Think about the favor of God this*
week and how it applies to your life. Choose one of the verses to write out below.

Dressed to Be Blessed

Joseph's doting Dad, Israel, also known as Jacob, provided a unique tunic for his favorite son. From the highly descriptive Hebrew, we learn that Joseph's tunic had long sleeves going past his wrists. It traveled all the way to his gangly, adolescent ankles. This colorful jacket was also highly decorated—you could see Joseph coming a mile down the dusty road.

Not only was Joseph's tunic beautiful, but it was also representative of Joseph's intimate relationship with his father. The type of robe Israel provided for Joseph was a garment of favoritism and of leadership. It was also associated with a high social and political status.

Your Father, because He loves you so dearly, has also provided a special tunic for you, just as Jacob did for Joseph. Your garment is multicolored and extraordinarily beautiful. The world should see you coming as you walk through storms, challenges, and disappointments in life, displaying your covering, provided through an intimate and loving relationship with your heavenly Dad. The tunic you have been given to wear throughout all of life is a garment of praise.

My friend, you are dressed and completely enveloped in the Father's love for you. The very first recognizable trait that others should observe about your life is how you are blanketed—from head to toe—in your worship of Him.

According to Hebraic tradition, the particular tunic Joseph was given by his father was used to signify two particular values: leadership and royalty. The garment bequeathed to you by your Father represents the same two values. You are a servant- leader because of your family heritage in Christ. And you are deemed as royalty not because of anything you have done, but because of who your spiritual Dad is.

Your Father longs for you to remove the sackcloth and ashes from your life, so He can dress you in a garment worthy of honor.

To grant to those who mourn in Zion,
Giving them a garland instead of ashes,
The oil of gladness instead of mourning,
The mantle of praise instead of a spirit of fainting.
So they will be called oaks of righteousness,
The planting of the Lord, that He may be glorified.

—Isaiah 61:3

You are completely covered in and identified by the tunic of praise the Father has given to you, simply because He is head over heels in love with you.

It has always interested as well as invigorated me, knowing the garment of praise was specifically given for times of mourning and fainting. During those difficult moments in life, our garment of praise should cover our lives completely, vividly prominent for the world around us to see. The prophet Isaiah, through the unction of the Holy Spirit, reminds us that when life is the most devastating, our praise should shout the loudest.

The Father knows what you and I often ignore—the only way to survive deep tragedy and undeserved pain is through the gift of worship. Praising God does not ignore our pain, but it enables us as His beloved children to process it in the healthiest way possible.

⧗ *The issue of pain and how we handle it as believers is a challenging one. Why do you believe the Father gave us the garment of praise for those exact moments in life?*

⧗ *Can you think of another passage in Scripture that might encourage you to worship when life is hard?*

⏳ *What other people in the Bible chose to worship, even when their circumstances were challenging?*

⏳ *What is your favorite worship song or hymn? Spend some time today listening to it, even singing along.*

⏳ *Write out 1 Peter 1:6–8 below.*

⏳ *I hope you have memorized our treasure verse for this week and that it has attached itself to your mind and spirit.*

What comes into our minds when we think about God is
the most important thing about us.

—A. W. Tozer
The Knowledge of the Holy

THE JOSEPH PRINCIPLE

Susanna Wesley

S usanna's father was a pastor, and she was the youngest in his brood of twenty-five children. When Susanna was only thirteen years old, she left her father's church because she disagreed with his theology, so astute was her study and her principles. At the age of nineteen, she married Samuel, who was seven years older than she. Together, they had nineteen children. Nine of her children died as infants. The tragic heartbreak of Susanna's life happened when one of her healthy babies was accidentally smothered by a young maid.

Susanna's husband, like her father, was a pastor. But he spent a large portion of his adult life in debtor's prison for mishandling the family finances. Their house burned down twice, and during the second fire, her son, John, was nearly killed. This gifted, opinionated, godly mother homeschooled all her children for six hours a day. She taught Greek, Latin, classical literature, math, and science in her family's school.

I am content to fill a little space if God be glorified.

—*Susanna Wesley*

Samuel left Susanna for nearly a year because of a disagreement in their marriage. He felt they should pray for the King of England, and she refused to pray for such a man. Susanna was unbending in her staunch beliefs and so rather than fight with her, Samuel decided to move out.

Faced with a life like Susanna's, most of us would crawl into a fetal position and stay covered in the blackness of well-deserved depression. However, what one *deserves* to choose and what one *should* choose are two different things entirely.

Susanna Wesley was known by all as a woman who held the Word of God in high esteem. Every day, regardless of what was going on in her home or in her life, she spent two hours of study in the Bible. In addition to the delight of reading the Scriptures, Susanna had a rich and vibrant prayer life, allowing nothing to interrupt it.

Susanna pastored the church held in the family home in her husband's absence—which was quite often—and people loved hearing her insight into the Scriptures. When Samuel was at home and able to pastor the church, attendance dwindled to nearly no one other than family. However, when Samuel was away and Susanna was given the opportunity to preach a lively sermon, the church increased to over two hundred.

Not only did Susanna pastor their church, teach the children, run the farm, and keep food on the table, but she was also a student of theology and scriptural commentaries. She wrote stunning and academic commentaries on the Apostles' Creed, the Ten Commandments, and the Lord's Prayer, all while raising her large and boisterous family.

This woman, Susanna Wesley, was an extraordinary combination of wit, compassion, opinion, and deep thinking. Most women forced to live her life of poverty, with an absentee and inattentive husband, a house filled with children, and the tragedy of losing nine offspring, would have given up living. But not Susanna Wesley. Susanna chose to stay engaged in the life she had been given and to live wholeheartedly for the Christ of the Gospels.

Eventually, two of her sons, John and Charles, brought revival to the newly birthed United States of America. They wrote hymns that are still widely sung today and their books are considered classical Christian theology and literature. John and Charles Wesley are esteemed as two of the most influential Christians of all time.

Susanna refused to be trapped by the quicksand of her devastating circumstances, instead choosing to love and obey God, even when her world was falling apart. Susanna held fast to God and His promises, despite deep emotional pain and rejection. The legacy of Susanna's life echoes through the centuries as a powerful testament to the blessing and abundance of God when one ordinary person chooses to love God unremittingly.

There are two things to do about the gospel.
Believe it and behave it.

—*Susanna Wesley*

Week 2

Jealous Hearts

Day 1

Dream God's Dream

His brothers saw that their father loved him more than all his brothers; and so they hated him and could not speak to him on friendly terms. **(Genesis 37:4)**

Preferential treatment by a parent to one specific child will never bode well in the dynamics of a family. Joseph was not spoiled in the true sense of the word because he was taught to be a hard worker and was given responsibility. However, Jacob showed his favoritism to Joseph by dressing him finer than he did the rest of his children. Jacob may have felt that Joseph deserved this privilege due to his work ethic or his heart attitude, but his brothers resented it intensely. When Joseph's brothers saw him wearing this coat, his brothers recognized it as a sign of their father's choice of Joseph as manager. They realized that Joseph would likely be in charge of them—his elder brothers.

But there is a deeper issue than preferential treatment to consider in this verse. The hearts of this sibling group and their vile treatment of Joseph warrants closer inspection.

One of the most difficult and irrational aspects of living as a Christ-follower is the cruel rejection and verbal persecution we often endure during the meanwhile moments in life. The stark truth is that as much as your Father loves you and has chosen you as His favorite, you do have an enemy of your soul. This enemy, Satan, has hidden himself in the systems and culture of this world we live in. He and his puny band of brothers despise the airspace assigned to you and can't stand the fact that you are living for Christ at your moment in history. So, don't allow your feelings to be hurt when the world chooses to ignore your contributions, mocks your belief system, and systematically bullies you for righteousness' sake. As a matter of fact, if you are in sync with the world, you are likely in direct opposition to the kingdom of God.

You adulteresses, do you not know that friendship with the world is hostility toward God? Therefore whoever wishes to be a friend of the world makes himself an enemy of God.

—James 4:4

⧗   *Have you ever been persecuted for righteousness' sake? Share about that situation.*

⧗   *How has God worked that situation together for good?*

⧗   *What was the good that came about in you due to the unfair treatment?*

Blessed are those who have been persecuted for the sake of righteousness,
for theirs is the kingdom of heaven.

—Matthew 5:10

Not One Kind Word

In Genesis 37:4, we learn that Joseph's brothers were unable to speak to him on friendly terms. One translation states, "They could not speak one kind word to Joseph." When I think of the character and potential that existed in the soul of the very young Joseph, this is outrageous to me. The nerve of these older brothers who only brought pain into the life of their little brother. What we have read thus far in the narrative has spotlighted a sad tale of separation, rejection, and unfair treatment. We will soon learn that the situation will grow worse—much worse—before it gets any better.

And isn't that the truth of the meanwhile in all our lives? It does indeed get worse before it gets better. Rejection compounds misery which magnifies soul pain which increases alienation which results in unhealthy behaviors. A meanwhile is often provoked by people, multiplied by time, and exacerbated by a lack of kindness.

⏳ *The Bible refers to the importance of the words we speak, often both in the Old Testament and New Testament. How do cruel words prolong a difficult situation in life?*

⏳ *How do kind words bring relief into a difficult situation?*

⏳ *Who do you know that is currently going through an unfair situation? How could you speak words of kindness to this person to bring encouragement to his or her life?*

A Dream

Joseph had two dreams that he felt compelled to share with his brothers. With the telling of these dreams, Joseph's brothers became even more annoyed with this young leader and dreamer. The intense but prophetic first dream did not build an intimacy with his brothers but added to their hate toward him.

> **Then Joseph had a dream, and when he told it to his brothers, they hated him even more. He said to them, "Please listen to this dream which I have had; for behold, we were binding sheaves in the field, and lo, my sheaf rose up and also stood erect; and behold, your sheaves gathered around and bowed down to my sheaf." Then his brothers said to him, "Are you actually going to reign over us? Or are you really going to rule over us?" So they hated him even more for his dreams and for his words. (Genesis 37:5–8)**

Joseph made no attempt to interpret, analyze, or give application to his dream. He simply related its stunning reality.

I believe all Christians are meant to dream the dreams of God, who is our good, good Father. I believe one of the many ways in which He speaks to His children is through the venue of dreams.

The brothers in the story of Joseph represent the world's opinion of Christ-followers. While we dream God-breathed dreams, the world doesn't care about them and ultimately may hate us for the dreams God has placed in our hearts. The world does not understand the language of Christianity which is the vernacular of God-inspired dreams.

⧖   *Has God ever spoken to you through dreams? Write one down here.*

⧖   *If God has never spoken to you through dreams, perhaps you would be bold enough to ask Him to speak to you, even tonight, while you are sleeping.*

I keep a small journal and a pen beside my bed so when I dream a particular dream that I perceive to be from God, I can write it down, even in the middle of the night. But perhaps you struggle to believe this could happen for you. Perhaps you, along with thousands of other women, think thoughts like these:

- But I am just a mom with lots of children. I don't have time for a dream.
- I am overweight and deeply in debt. Certainly, God doesn't have any magnificent plans for my life.
- I am uneducated . . . depressed . . . divorced.

My friend, stop giving God your excuses and give Him your heart. Give Him your availability and your time. Give God your future.

Some of you might think you are too old to dream a new dream for the advancement of God's kingdom. If you feel you are a used up, beat up old relic, let me remind you that Corrie ten Boom was in her fifties when she hid Jews from the Nazis. She was in her sixties, seventies, and eighties when she traveled the world for the Lord.

Caleb, of the Old Testament, was eighty-five years old when he asked God to give him another mountain and more battles to fight (Joshua 14:6–12).

God doesn't merely utilize the vigor of the young as He is about to do with Joseph. He also uses those who deeply desire to play a significant role in the economy of God's kingdom, after life has provided plentiful amounts of time, experience, and wisdom.

Remember, you are Joseph in this story and God has dreams for you to dream, regardless of your age.

⏳   *Have you asked God to use you right now at this moment in your life?*

⏳   *Are you brave enough to ask God for another mountain like Caleb did?*

⏳   *What dream has God placed in your heart?*

Hidden Treasure: Read this verse out loud several times today and write it out on a 3x5 card. Think about this verse throughout the week and begin to commit it to memory:

> *"For I know the plans that I have for you," declares the Lord,*
> *"plans for welfare and not for calamity to give you a*
> *future and a hope."*
>
> *Jeremiah 29:11*

> *Dreams carried around in one's heart for years, if they are dreams*
> *that have God's approval, have a way of suddenly*
> *materializing.*
>
> *—Catherine Marshall*
> *A Man Called Peter*

Day 2

A Dream and a Promise

Now he had still another dream, and related it to his brothers, and said, "Lo, I have had still another dream; and behold, the sun and the moon and eleven stars were bowing down to me." He related it to his father and to his brothers; and his father rebuked him and said to him, "What is this dream that you have had? Shall I and your mother and your brothers actually come to bow ourselves down before you to the ground?" His brothers were jealous of him, but his father kept the saying in mind. (Genesis 37:9–11)

The second dream given to Joseph caused an even greater rift among the sons of Jacob. It did not restore or even neutralize the relationship his brothers were wrestling with. The dress and the dreams of Joseph were insufferably exasperating to his brothers, and it became too much for them to bear. After the telling of the second dream, his father gently corrected him and wondered if Joseph was expecting preferential treatment from his family. Joseph's brothers were jealous and hateful toward him. Although Jacob, Joseph's father, doesn't feel about his son the way the older brothers feel, he will remember what Joseph has presented. Just as Mary, the mother of Jesus, treasured certain events of the life of Jesus in her heart (Luke 2:19, 51), Jacob, the father of Joseph, will remember the dreams of his extraordinary son.

The biblical text is silent on the motivation of Joseph in sharing his dreams with his family. Some assume it was youthful arrogance while others assert it was naiveté on Joseph's part. As I study the scope of Joseph's life and how he acted in other situations, I must say I believe it was because he believed the dreams were from God and therefore he held the responsibility of sharing them.

⧗ *Why do you believe Joseph shared these dreams with his family?*

Historical Perspective

The enemy, who runs rampant in the culture and systems of this fallen world, is jealous of your potential and will do absolutely anything to derail you from what God wants for your life. Even your biggest, most gargantuan dreams are minute in comparison to the dreams that God, your Father, has for you. What the world hates, heaven will applaud. What the culture dismantles, the Father will restore. What the enemy destroys, the Lord will breathe new life into again and again.

These verses in Genesis 37 are, of course, prophetic concerning the future of Joseph. Although Joseph's brothers were immediately and intensely offended, we know Joseph was only referencing what God had spoken to him. His brothers were livid, and his father disgruntled. We, however, are privy to the historical perspective of this riveting account.

⧖   *What does it mean to you to be the beneficiary of historical perspective?*

Did you know you have historical perspective concerning your life as well? You don't need to panic, embrace anger, be disgruntled, or feel frustrated with the events of your life as they unfold. You have been given historical perspective based upon the promises in the Bible. When things happen that you do not understand, situations you would not have chosen, and that seem grossly unfair to you, you can tap into historical perspective. You might wonder how that is even possible, but the unalterable truth of Romans 8:28 makes it clear.

> *And we know that God causes all things to work together for good to those who love God, to those who are called according to His purpose.*

⧖   *How will historical perspective change the way you treat people?*

⧖   *How will historical perspective influence your daily choices?*

There was a reason I presented the end of the story of Joseph at the beginning of our study. I wanted to assure you that God was working for Joseph from the very first day he was belittled by his brothers. You can also know, beyond a shadow of a doubt, that God is on your side, and He is working behind the scenes of your life as well. God is taking every ill intent, every difficult relationship, every lack you have suffered, every physical challenge you have faced, and He is "machashab-ing" it to work for your good.

What must you do to tap into this too-good-to-be-true promise of Romans 8:28? You must love the Lord and keep pressing into His wonderful purposes for your life. No matter what you are going through today just keep reminding yourself, *I have historical perspective. I know that all things will ultimately work together for my good. God has promised it and I believe it.*

⧗   *What does it mean in a practical sense to love the Lord?*

⧗   *What does it mean to be called according to His purposes?*

⧗   *Spend some time meditating on our treasure verse of the week. Look for an opportunity to share it with someone.*

The peace of our souls does not have to rise and fall with unpredictable people or situations. Our feelings will shift, of course. People do affect us. But the peace of our souls is tethered to all that God is. And though we can't predict His specific plans, the fact that God will work everything for good is a completely predictable promise.

—Lysa TerKeurst
Uninvited

Day 3

Better Times and Brighter Days

Then his brothers went to pasture their father's flock in Shechem. Israel said to Joseph, "Are not your brothers pasturing the flock in Shechem? Come, and I will send you to them." And he said to him, "I will go." Then he said to him, "Go now and see about the welfare of your brothers and the welfare of the flock, and bring word back to me." So he sent him from the valley of Hebron, and he came to Shechem. (Genesis 37:12–14)

Joseph was sent by his father, Israel also known as Jacob, to see if all was well with his older brothers who were shepherding the family flock somewhere near Shechem. One detail of this passage so dear to my heart is Joseph's response to his father's request. Joseph immediately replied, "I will go." The literal translation of this phrase from the Hebrew *hineni* is "Here I am." Joseph was telling his beloved father, "Dad, I am at your service. Whatever you ask of me, I will do. Wherever you send me, I will go."

Some Bible scholars translate this phrase as, "I am ready."[4]

If we are to read this scripture personally and thereby apply its theme to our lives, we must search our hearts and remember how we have replied to our heavenly Father when He has asked something difficult of us. Are you ready, like Joseph, to go wherever the Father sends you?

When the Lord asks one of us to work in the church nursery or teach Sunday school, we must respond, "I will go."

When the Lord asks one of us to be kind to a difficult person, we must respond, "Yes, Lord."

When the Lord requests that we give money to a missionary, a person, or a ministry, we must respond, "I will do it."

When the Lord lays it on one of our hearts to be a foster parent, our instant response should be, "I am ready."

⏳ *What has the Lord asked of you lately? What has your response been?*

Joseph traveled about fifty miles to find his siblings, presumably in Shechem, which was likely a three-day journey from their home. However, Joseph was unable to find his brothers when he arrived in Shechem.

⧗   *Do you have conflict in your family?*

⧗   *How do you handle that conflict?*

⧗   *What do you believe is the healthiest way to handle family dysfunction?*

A Happenstance

Joseph thoroughly scoured the fields where his big, unpredictable brothers had planned to shepherd the family flock, but the band of brothers was nowhere to be found. There did, however, just "happen" to be a man passing by who just "happened" to hear a conversation in which the older brothers had decided to move on to Dothan.

> *A man found him, and behold, Joseph was wandering in the field; and the man asked him, "What are you looking for?" He said, "I am looking for my brothers; please tell me where they are pasturing the flock." Then the man said, "They have moved from here, for I heard them say, 'Let us go to Dothan.'" So Joseph went after his brothers and found them at Dothan. (Genesis 37:15–17)*

Some theologians wonder if this referenced man was an angel of the Lord sent to help Joseph find his jealous brothers. Whether or not this man was a human being taking a walk or an angel sent by God, the unseen hand of the Lord is apparent in these details. The Lord is directing Joseph to locate his brothers so the divine plan for saving many people will be set into motion. God will draw much good from this one conversation that Joseph had with an anonymous man outside of Shechem. Joseph has this man to either thank or curse for pointing him toward Dothan.

Whether this man was truly an angel or just a man who "happened" to be in the right place at the opportune time, we will never know this side of heaven. What we do know, however, is that God is well able to send an angel to instigate His plans for humanity.

> *Do not neglect to show hospitality to strangers, for by this some have entertained angels without knowing it.*
>
> *—Hebrews 13:2*

⧗ *Have you ever been visited by someone and wondered if they were truly a human being or perhaps a divine messenger?*

⧗ *Do you believe it is possible that the Lord still uses his angels today to do His bidding? Why or why not?*

Here Comes the Dreamer

Shechem was an important city filled with people—large cities are much easier to get lost in than small, rural communities. Dothan, by this time in history, was already an ancient city who had seen better times and brighter days.

> **When they saw him from a distance and before he came close to them, they plotted against him to put him to death. (Genesis 37:18)**

⧗ *List three things we know Joseph's brothers have against him:*

1. _____

2. _____

3. _____

The multicolored garment that Joseph was likely wearing enabled his brothers to spot him when he was still at a great distance. You could see this kid a mile away because he was covered from his young neck to his fingertips to his feet in a coat that shouted of love, care, and leadership. His brothers didn't like it—they didn't like it one little bit. These ten angry men wasted no time in venting their anger against the younger Joseph, knowing he was away from the safety of home and the protection of Daddy. Suddenly, Joseph became fair game for their animosity. They were not expecting Joseph to visit them and so the murder they plotted was not so much premeditated as it was reactive, yet still fed by slow-burning hatred.

I wonder what they began to speak as Joseph in his telling tunic drew closer.

"Here he comes. Daddy's little spoiled brat!"

"Here comes the big talker! I wonder what dream he's the main character in now?"

"He thinks he's such big stuff but really he is a big, fat loser! And we are stuck with him!"

Finally, these angry and jealous brothers began to plot the demise of Joseph, their father's favorite son.

They said to one another, "Here comes this dreamer!" (Genesis 37:19)

Although I can imagine that they said other unkind phrases about Joseph, the Bible only tells us of one phrase, "Here comes this dreamer!" This was the very worst the angry men could declare about their younger, favored sibling. Apparently, Joseph had not been unkind to them, he wasn't selfish, nor was he a whiner. Joseph was only a truth-teller. The Hebrew translates this phrase with blatant sarcasm and a correct translation might lean more toward "master dreamer."[5]

Isn't it interesting that apparently the one characteristic they hated the most about Joseph was his penchant for dreaming? They didn't say they hated him because his daddy loved him, nor did they say they despised Joseph due to his gorgeous and expensive coat. They didn't say they couldn't stand the sight of Joseph because he had reported their mistakes to their father. These grown men hated Joseph because of his grandiose dreams given to Him by God. They abhorred Joseph due to his ability to hear from God and to know that God had a bright future for him.

⏳   *Have you ever been the victim of gossip or of bullying?*

⧖   *Have you forgiven those who have targeted your life with their words?*

⧖   *Is there anyone you need to ask forgiveness from due to gossip that came from your mouth?*

The Gift of Hope

As you walk down the road of life, covered from head to toe in the Father's great love for you, live in a manner that ensures the world has nothing of which to accuse you.

Joseph's brothers, in the natural, had left the healthy city of Shechem for the dying town of Dothan. Even their geographical location symbolically spoke of the state of their hearts.

Joseph was intent on living his life by faith and the eternal truth that God is good and that He had unmatched plans for Joseph's one singular life. His brothers, who traveled in a pack, were wolf-like in their approach to relationship. These intimidated brothers had moved from a place of productivity and possibility to an ancient village of ruts, ruins, and run-down plans.

What is the desire of your heart? Do you want to travel to Dothan? Or would you prefer to be known as a dreamer? It's up to you. Isn't it interesting that when we truly embrace a historical perspective based upon the promises of God that our hearts and minds are set resolutely to the future? It's the gift of hope.

⧖   *Spend time today meditating on the treasure verse for the week.*

⧖   *What are three plans you hope to accomplish during your life on earth?*

To wait with openness and trust is an enormously radical attitude toward life. It is choosing to hope that something is happening for us that is far beyond our own imaginings. It is giving up control over our future and letting God define our life. It is living with the conviction that God molds us in love, holds us in tenderness, and moves us away from the sources of our fear.

Our spiritual life is a life in which we wait, actively present to the moment, expecting that new things will happen to us, new things that are far beyond our own imagination or prediction. This, indeed, is a very radical stance toward life in a world preoccupied with control.

—*Henri Nouwen*
Finding My Way Home

Day 4

---

10 Angry Men

"Now then, come and let us kill him and throw him into one of the pits; and we will say, 'A wild beast devoured him.' Then let us see what will become of his dreams!" **(Genesis 37:20)**

This turn of events in Scripture is nearly unbelievable. How did this family go from mere jealousy over the dreams of a teenaged boy to embracing volatile anger, ultimately moving to murderous intent?

As Joseph's older brothers saw him walking down the road from Shechem to Dothan, they refused to stand up and greet him. It never crossed their bitter minds to walk toward him, offer him a meal, a place to sit, or to ask about their father. We are about to study one of the cruelest happenings, other than the death of Christ, recorded in Scripture. We read of other murders and of army fighting against army, but there is nowhere else in the Bible where we are confronted with a gang mentality, especially among brothers. These ten angry men had allowed resentment and grudges to grow in their hearts and it consumed their perspective in every way possible.

Bitterness and Jealousy

One of the most valiant and necessary battles we all must fight is to guard against a root of bitterness. If we allow disgruntlement to take over the garden of our hearts, bitterness will grow rampantly. It will cause trouble and many people will be negatively impacted by it. I love the way The Passion Translation of the Bible presents this soul-searching verse:

Be carefully on your guard lest there be any one who falls back from the grace of God; lest any root bearing bitter fruit spring up and cause trouble among you, and through it the whole brotherhood be defiled.

—Hebrews 12:15 Weymouth

It isn't always easy to shine biblical truth on our twenty-first-century lives, but it's always healing. When you consider Joseph's brothers, can you relate to their feelings at all? How would you answer the following?

⧗ *Have you ever been jealous of someone?*

⧗ *Are you jealous of someone today?*

⧗ *How does jealousy cause you to act?*

Bitterness is not to be juggled like a play toy nor is it to be embraced like a close friend. We should always shun bitterness quickly, deal with it, and perpetually remove it. In the life of Joseph's brothers, bitterness grew from the seed of their jealousy.

His brothers were jealous of him. (Genesis 37:11)

⧗ *What is the difference between bitterness and jealousy?*

⧗ *Which emotion—bitterness or jealousy—is more dangerous? Explain your answer.*

Jealousy is an evil and wicked emotion and should never be tolerated or placated in the life of a Christian. Envy or jealousy can be defined as the antagonism or enmity that is produced by someone else's blessing or favorable circumstances. Jealousy is innately destructive and like hidden dynamite it will blow up a person's life quickly.

---

*For where jealousy and selfish ambition exist, there
is disorder and every evil thing.*

—James 3:16

Jealousy, at its core, resents what God has done in the life of someone else. A jealous person is angry with God for the blessings He has bestowed upon another. Donald Barnhouse, the writer and theologian has said, "When a man is covetous and envious, he is saying, 'God, I am not satisfied; you didn't give me what I want.'"[6]

When jealousy rules and reigns in our human hearts, we are attempting to de-throne God and make decisions that only God has the authority to make. Jealousy seeks to exalt self and makes way for bitterness.

⧖   *How does it make you feel to realize that jealousy is an attempt to use God's authority for our own self-benefit?*

The Cure

Bitterness and envy will cause you to act in ways contrary to God's nature and His perfect will for your life. They will drive you to say and do things that will cause havoc and destruction everywhere you go. The healthier alternative is to bless those who have been blessed by the Father and to encourage those who are in positions of leadership or authority. The most vital decision a disciple of Christ can make when faced with envious feelings is to cultivate a spirit of thanksgiving. Rather than exhibit the destructive weed of jealousy, determine today that you will always celebrate others for their accomplishments and blessings.

⧖   *List at least five things for which you are grateful today.*

Joseph's brothers were driven to murder Joseph and kill his dreams or his potential. Rather than allowing Joseph to fulfill God's plans for his life, they sought to destroy him.

⏳ *Spend some time memorizing this week's treasure verse. How does this verse help you deal with jealousy?*

---

*Always remember that God's control is behind
everything. His care encircles every incident and
event of our lives. This means that we can maintain an
attitude of perfect trust in him and an eagerness
to ask God for aid in our daily living.*

*—Oswald Chambers
Devotions for a Deeper Life*

Preparing for Challenges

This week's lesson has been a challenging one, hasn't it? Unfortunately, we must address the difficult issues that the life story of Joseph introduces. We must also examine our own lives in the eternal light of Scripture. We simply must.

As I contemplate the evil in the hearts of Joseph's brothers, provoked by jealousy, I also ponder this verse:

> *Men of bloodshed hate the blameless,*
> *But the upright are concerned for his life.*
>
> —*Proverbs 29:10*

I do not hold a murderous weapon in my hand, and that fact alone is magnanimous. But I must also take myself to the next level by supporting and celebrating the emotional and spiritual lives of those around me. You see, merely choosing not to assassinate someone's character or not to incriminate the human object of my jealousy is simply not enough.

I must be concerned for the life of the person whose blessings and perspective have aggravated the infection of bitterness in me. I must join my heart to the heart of the challenging person, feel what they are feeling, and then wish them well. I must be thankful for what God has done for this outstanding person and even pray for him or her and bless them with my lips. But first, I must face the truth of my own heart.

⧗   *Who have you felt evil against that the Lord is now leading you to bless?*

⧗   *What will you specifically do for this person?*

⧗ *As you reread Proverbs 29:10, compare the words hate and concerned. Write down the differences in meaning between these two words below.*

God Sees

As I contemplate the stirring fact that the only accusation the brothers could use to bully Joseph was that he was a dreamer, I must not ignore the truth that his dreams were God's way of preparing both Joseph and his brothers for a future reality. God has a magnificent way of preparing His chosen people for both trials and blessings they cannot yet see. God saw ahead into the decades of Joseph's life and prepared him for leadership. However, although Joseph dreamed of his future authority, he certainly did not dream of his imprisonment. Generally, when a young man dreams a dream or a young lady sees a vision, their gaze is set on prosperity and pleasure rather than on trouble and discipline. And yet, this is where growth happens.

⧗ *What is a dream you had as a young person? Did this dream prepare you for challenges or only for possibilities?*

⧗ *What is the dream of your heart today? Write it out.*

The Christ-Figure

You may have guessed by now that Joseph is a type of Christ-figure in this story of drama, intrigue, and human pain. Although Joseph was the beloved son of his father, he was hated by a wicked world just like Jesus was. Jesus came from heaven to seek after us and to save us just as Joseph was sent to seek after his own brothers. His brothers did not receive him but chose a malicious plot instead. Similarly, God used the evil intended for Jesus to save all the generations to come—those who would accept His forgiveness and love.

*Fixing our eyes on Jesus, the author and perfecter of faith,
who for the joy set before Him endured the cross, despising
the shame, and has sat down at the right hand of
the throne of God.*

— *Hebrews 12:2*

Although the above scripture is describing what Jesus went through, we can also apply it to Joseph's life. Joseph realized there was a "joy set before him" due to the dreams he had been given. However, he had to develop the muscle of endurance before he experienced the joy. God has a way of preparing His people beforehand, just as He did with Joseph and Jesus, for trials we are unable to predict.

Many evangelical theologians believe the foreshadowing of Christ can be found in every book of the Bible. In Genesis, the character of Joseph assures us that God will have the last word. The coming of Christ was not for naught but to save us from our own sins. Let's consider how this impacts us today.

⏳ *How do you see Joseph as a Christ-figure in this story?*

⏳ *Have you ever led anyone to Christ?*

⏳ *Take the time now to write out a prayer of salvation you could pray over someone whom you might lead to Christ. It pays to be prepared.*

⧗   *Make sure you share this week's treasure verse with someone in your life.*

---

*The cure for the sin of envy and jealousy is to
find our contentment in God.*

—Jerry Bridges
The Pursuit of Holiness

THE JOSEPH PRINCIPLE

Betty Scott Stam

Lord, I give up all my own plans and purposes, all my own desires and hopes, and accept Thy will for my life. I give myself, my life, my all utterly to Thee to be Thine forever. Fill me and seal me with Thy Holy Spirit. Use me as Thou wilt, send me where Thou wilt and work out Thy whole will in my life at any cost now and forever.

This was the prayer Betty Scott, as an earnest teenager, prayed during her first year of college. It was shortly after this she met a young man, John Stam, while attending Moody Bible Institute in Chicago. They were married in 1933, when John was twenty-six and Betty was twenty-seven, and they served as missionaries in the Anhui province of China. During the day, they visited nearby villages to share the gospel—in the evenings, they helped to lead meetings with another missionary in the region. The work was difficult, as the area was mountainous and the people extremely poor, but the Stams rejoiced at the opportunity God had given them to share the good news of Christ.

On September 11, 1934, their daughter, Helen Priscilla, was born.

John and Betty rented a storefront where they both lived and held services for the people in the village. The Stams were not the first white missionary couple to visit this village, but they were the first to make it their home.

On the morning of December 6, 1934, when baby Helen was only three months old, there was a knock at the front door of the storefront. Betty was bathing the baby and the messenger at the door announced to John that Communist bandits were on their way to the village. The young Stam family immediately made preparations to leave, but it was already too late. Encouraged by the wild cheering of the people in the village, the bandits broke through the front door of the Stam's home. They were told to take off their clothes and leave only in their undergarments.

The first night they were taken to the local prison where the other prisoners graciously made room for the young family. When baby Helen started to cry, one of the other Christian prisoners asked the guards to at least allow someone to leave with the baby. This prisoner was hacked to death in front of Betty and John and their crying infant.

The following morning, December 7, 1934, John's hands were tightly bound behind his back and Betty was allowed to walk beside him carrying their baby girl. They marched twelve miles in the bitter cold and then were thrust into a mud hut to spend the night. Their captors unbound John's hands and he was given the opportunity to write a letter. This is the letter he wrote to the mission board while in captivity:

> My wife, baby, and myself are today in the hands of Communist bandits. Whether we will be released or not no one knows. May God be magnified in our bodies, whether by life or by death. Philippians 1:20[7]

Sometime during that cold, dark night, Betty looked for the last time at the angelic face of her sleeping daughter and nursed her for one last moment. Then Betty bundled Helen inside her blanket and hid her under the covers with two five-dollar bills. The bandits came for John and Betty in the early morning hours of December 8, 1934.

They were marched down the streets of Miaosheo to their deaths while curious onlookers lined both sides of the streets. A compassionate Chinese shopkeeper boldly walked out of the crowd and tried to persuade the Communists not to kill the Stams. The aggressive soldiers ordered the man to go back into his shop; however, he quietly refused. The soldiers then plundered the home of the shopkeeper and found a Chinese copy of the Holy Bible as well as a well-worn hymnbook. The shopkeeper was then bound and led with the Stams to death for the crime of being a Christian.

After marching to the center of the village, John was ordered to kneel. In one swoop of the Chinese sword he was violently beheaded. Betty and the shopkeeper were killed seconds later.

A courageous Christian, Mr. Lo, had followed the bandits who beheaded John and Betty Stam and the village shopkeeper. When Mr. Lo came upon the gruesome scene, he obtained help from the underground Christian community and placed all three bodies in coffins. Mr. Lo then went to look for the three-month-old baby girl who was still missing. He retraced the steps of the entourage to the mud hut and although over twenty-four hours had passed since Betty and John Stam had left their baby girl, she was smiling and happy under the pile of blankets where her mother had hidden this precious little life. Mr. Lo transported baby Helen to her maternal grandparents who were also missionaries in China.

John Stam had sent a poem to his father, Peter, who had been concerned about their safety in the Chinese village. John's wisdom and perseverance are illustrated in these poignant yet powerful lines by E. H. Hamilton:

"Afraid? Of what?
To feel the spirit's glad release?
To pass from pain to perfect peace,
the strife and strain of life to cease?
Afraid—of that?

Afraid? Of what?
Afraid to see the Savior's face,
To hear His welcome, and to trace
the glory gleam from wounds of grace?
Afraid—of that?

Afraid? Of what?
A flash—a crash—a pierced heart;
Darkness—Light—O Heaven's art?
A wound of His a counterpart!
Afraid? Of that?

Afraid? Of what?
To do by death what life could not –
Baptize with blood a stony plot,
Till souls shall blossom from the spot?
Afraid? Of that?[8]

The coffins of the three martyrs stayed on the hillside of the remote village for forty days until the government released them for burial. Mr. Lo had lovingly sewn their heads back on their earthly bodies and when the caskets were opened nearly a month and a half after their deaths, John and Betty were still clothed in only their underwear. But Mr. Lo wrapped them in white linen, covering both of their faces, smiling with expectancy.

John and Betty Stam's bodies were buried on a hillside. Their gravestones read:

John Cornelius Stam
January 18, 1907
"That Christ may be glorified whether by life or death."
Philippians 1:20

Elisabeth Scott Stam
February 22, 1906
"For me to live is Christ and to die is gain."
Philippians 1:21

On December 8, 1943, perhaps John and Betty Stam looked beyond the hate and anger of their assassins and saw Christ's lovely face and were greeted by the joy of His presence.

When we consecrate ourselves to God, we think we are making a great sacrifice, and doing lots for Him, when really we are only letting go of some little bitsy trinkets we have been grabbing, and when our hands are empty, He fills them full of His treasure.

—Betty Stam

Week 3

The End
of the Beginning

Day 1

Pleasing People or Pleasing God?

A re you a people pleaser? How do you make the difficult, heart-wrenching decisions in life when other people's opinions are involved? Let's once again eavesdrop on the conversation among Joseph's brothers and strive to discern why this brood of siblings seemed void of human kindness.

> *But Reuben heard this and rescued him out of their hands and said, "Let us not take his life." Reuben further said to them, "Shed no blood. Throw him into this pit that is in the wilderness, but do not lay hands on him"—that he might rescue him out of their hands, to restore him to his father.* (Genesis 37:21–22)

At first glance, one might applaud Reuben and suppose that he is trying to save the life of Joseph. But as I study these Scriptures and the ones that follow, I wonder if Reuben is merely being a "people-pleaser," trying to supplicate his angry and vicious brothers.

Reuben was the eldest son, and he should have been the gracious leader of the group. Reuben should have definitively called an immediate end to their barbaric plans. If anyone possessed a backbone of strength and honor, it should have been Reuben. Now, I will admit that not all commentaries agree with me on this point. However, even though Reuben does stand up for Joseph, he is largely overruled and so his leadership must not have been as strong or as wise as one would expect of the elder brother.

Perhaps Reuben did intend to save Joseph, but his plan failed. Reuben suggested they place him in a pit in the wilderness rather than kill him. Whether these violent men murdered Joseph on the spot or chose the lesser of two evils which was to throw him into a waterless, desert pit, certainly their motive was jealousy. The action would result in sin. As you ponder the violent choices by these groveling, pugnacious brothers, consider this verse as a cleansing tool to rid us of the compromise of jealousy and bitterness:

Do nothing from selfishness or empty conceit, but with humility of mind regard one another as more important than yourselves; do not merely look out for your own personal interests, but also for the interests of others. Have this attitude in yourselves which was also in Christ Jesus, who, although He existed in the form of God, did not regard equality with God a thing to be grasped, but emptied Himself, taking the form of a bond-servant, and being made in the likeness of men. Being found in appearance as a man, He humbled Himself by becoming obedient to the point of death, even death on a cross.

— Philippians 2:3–8

⧖   According to this verse, when are you allowed to be selfish?

⧖   Are you allowed to look out for your personal interests? What is the caveat in looking out for your own interests?

⧖   What is the attitude Christ embraced that we, too, are instructed to exhibit?

Stand Up

Taking a stand for what is right and of the highest good is never an easy choice, but it is always the only decision. I pray that you, as a daughter of Christ, will choose to demonstrate a backbone of truth and virtue. When someone is mistreated or bullied, speak up for justice and decency. Refuse to be a mere people-pleaser with the one extraordinary life you have been given. Stand up for the underdog, cheer for the unfortunate, and give to the oppressed. Whether it is the preborn, those whose skin is a different color than yours, or someone of a different political persuasion, never join in with the voices of Joseph's brothers. Stand alone, if you must, but stand up for all that is good, compassionate, and merciful.

⌛ *What cause do you feel you could give time or prayer to?*

⌛ *Do you have friends whose skin tone is different from yours? Whose political persuasion is different? Who are of a different socioeconomic level?*

Hold On to It

The first action Joseph's brothers took against the unsuspecting young man was stripping him of his colorful garment. Remember, this robe symbolized the garment of praise we have been given by our Father, to carry us through our difficult days. When you are being attacked by Satan, the enemy of your soul, the first thing he will try to do is strip you of your garment of praise. The devil often deals in our emotional responses, using them to corrupt our desire to worship.

> **So it came about, when Joseph reached his brothers, that they stripped Joseph of his tunic, the varicolored tunic that was on him. (Genesis 37:23)**

The brightly colored garment Joseph wore was also a robe of leadership and royalty. If the enemy can convince you to take off your garment of praise, he can better attack you with lies concerning your identity. You might begin to consider the untruth that the Father doesn't really care about you and that He has forgotten you. But worship, the human response to the love of the Father, protects us. Worship chooses to sing the songs of faith that thousands have sung before us. We do not worship God based upon our circumstances or because of our desires but based upon our relationship with our Father.

⌛ *What has the enemy tried to steal from you when you were unsuspecting?*

⧖   *How is our choice to worship the Father also tied into our identity in Christ?*

⧖   *Why is it important not to lose your song when life is difficult?*

Hidden Treasure: Read this verse out loud several times today and write it out on a 3x5 card. Think about this verse throughout the week and begin to commit it to memory:

> *To grant those who mourn in Zion,*
> *Giving them a garland instead of ashes,*
> *The oil of gladness instead of mourning,*
> *The mantle of praise instead of a spirit of fainting.*
> *So they will be called oaks of righteousness,*
> *The planting of the Lord, that He may be glorified.*
>
> —Isaiah 61:3

Sometimes I go to God and say, "God, if Thou dost never answer another prayer while I live on this earth, I will still worship Thee as long as I live and in the ages to come for what Thou hast done already. God's already put me so far in debt that if I were to live one million millenniums I couldn't pay Him for what He's done for me."

—A. W. Tozer
Worship

Day 2

The Pit

And they took him and threw him into the pit. Now the pit was empty, without any water in it. (Genesis 37:24)

A s we study the meaning behind some of the words in this chapter of Genesis, we will discover that Joseph's older brothers fully intended to kill him.

"Now then, come and let us kill him and throw him into one of the pits." (Genesis 37:20)

Reuben further said to them, "Shed no blood. Throw him into this pit." (Genesis 37:22)

The Hebrew word for "throw," used in past and present tense in all three of the above verses, did not mean to toss or to fling. It was the Hebrew word *salak*. *Salak* was always—not sometimes but always—used in conjunction with the placing of a dead body in a grave. The brothers intended for Joseph to die in the pit. They were certain the pit would become his grave.

Joseph's brothers threw him in a dried-up cistern. Dothan was a dying city and these cisterns were likely decrepit and no longer used by the dwindling population. A cistern was shaped much like a bottle with a small opening on top, often covered with a larger stone. Cisterns, during this time in history, were hewn into the rock and only had a narrow, vertical shaft at the top, used for letting down pitchers. If a human being fell into a cistern, their chances of being extracted alive were minimal. Joseph was forcefully impelled into a dry, confining place meant to become his casket. He was left to die under the ground, in darkness, alone with no hope of rescue. His brothers had left him in an abyss, a vacuous place. Because the walls of the cistern were hewn into the rock, Joseph would never be able to claw his way to the top. Although the brothers were restrained from murdering him, without the intervention of God, Joseph was sure to die nonetheless.

⧗   *What is one negative emotion you struggle with in life?*

⧗   *How does that emotion sometimes keep you in the pit?*

You Don't Deserve It!

The state in which Joseph found himself at this juncture in his story is no different from the place where the enemy wants you to remain. The devil is known for throwing people into dry pits where it feels like there is no hope of coming out alive. David, the songwriter, giant-killer, and king, knew this pit well.

I am reckoned among those who go down to the pit;
I have become like a man without strength.

Psalm 88:4

The enemy of your soul has a plan for your life—and it is a dastardly one. He has come to "steal and kill and destroy" (John 10:10). His ugly plan is that you, as a believer in Christ, will live out your earthly days in the pit of despair, the pit of hopelessness, or the pit of unending depression. There is no vital sustenance in the pit the enemy has planned for you nor is there any potential for growth or nourishment. The devil is unable to take eternal life from you and so he endeavors to take abundant life from you.

⧗   *What does the pit in the story of Joseph symbolize to you?*

Joseph had done absolutely nothing to deserve being thrown into this hopeless, black, dry place. Oh, he had dreamed a few dreams, but they were given to him by God. He had perhaps been guilty of youthful enthusiasm and of enjoying his treasured place in his father's heart, but Joseph certainly did not deserve the pit—and neither do you.

Get Out of That Pit

You might feel you are merely existing in life and have spent way too much time in the pit, where a lack of self-worth surrounds you in darkness. But remind yourself today that no one—including you and Joseph—deserves to live their life in the pit. If you take off your garment of praise, you might land in the abyss of discouragement and melancholy. Perhaps it is time for you to climb up the ladder, worship, and get out of that pit.

⏳ *Do you believe it is possible to "sing your way out of the pit"?*

You have an enemy—just like Joseph did—and your enemy intends to "salak" you into the pit so you will die in that wretched, lifeless place. You might not literally die in the pit, but your future could quickly become a skeleton of undreamed dreams. Your joy could cease to be vibrant, causing your strength to fade away. So today, purpose in your heart that you will sing, even when in the trench of pain, sorrow, or despondency. Joseph's days in the pit were numbered—and so are yours!

⏳ *One of the ways I have been helped out of the pit of depression is to encourage someone else, listen to worship music, read my Bible, or even go for a walk. Make a list of the ways you can lift yourself out of the pit:*

1. _____

2. _____

3. _____

4. _____

⧗ *Spend some time memorizing our treasure verse for the week. As you read it over,*
meditate on it and allow the meaning to lift you out of the pit.

There is no pit so deep that He is not deeper still.

—*Corrie ten Boom*
The Hiding Place

Day 3

A Caravan Is on Its Way!

J oseph's brothers initially experienced no remorse after throwing their younger sibling into the dry, narrow pit. What did this dysfunctional band of brothers do next? Read on.

Then they sat down to eat a meal. (Genesis 37:25)

These brothers were so desperately evil and cold-hearted that after they roughed up Joseph, stole his clothes, and threw him into an empty, black pit, they sat down to dine. Have these men no hearts? No hearts at all? I can picture it now. Perhaps Simeon smacked his lips while Dan burped and slurped. Maybe Levi pushed Judah aside to get a second portion while Asher cut off a large chunk of meat that had been cooked over the fire. The barbarity of these brothers allowed them to feast on the provisions Joseph had brought to them from their giving father.

Later in the story of Joseph, we will learn that he cried out in distress to his brothers when they threw him into the cistern. Joseph begged for his life, and yet his brothers ignored him and munched on the happy meal Daddy had sent from afar. I hope those of you who have been abused, mistreated, rejected, and ignored will find this portion of Scripture deeply moving as well as comforting. I know you will be able to identify with Joseph as he cried out for compassion from his heartless brothers. I hope as the story of Joseph continues to gloriously unfold, you will commit your experience to God, who heard your heartbroken cries, and who always moves to restore and rescue.

But I must not move past this section without painting yet another word picture for those of you who are reading from the grandstand of ease and comfort. Take a deep breath . . . look around you . . . listen for someone's cries. We dare not eat simply because we are comfortable while a hurting Joseph is crying. Do you hear it? Do you hear the sobs of a Joseph? What will you do about it?

God Always Hears

Interestingly enough, this is the last recorded time in Joseph's story when his self-centered and vengeful brothers will enjoy a meal without the absolute provision of Joseph. A day is coming when their daily sustenance will depend solely upon the kindness of Joseph. God watched this scenario unfold knowing He would someday settle the score. Do not surmise that God doesn't love you or that He is not aware of your pain just because others have used you or even abused you. Give God time. He is on your side just like He was with Joseph.

> *Never take your own revenge, beloved, but leave room*
> *for the wrath of God, for it is written, "Vengeance is Mine,*
> *I will repay," says the Lord.*
>
> *—Romans 12:19*

⌛ *What is your definition of the word* kindness?

⌛ *As Christ-followers, why is it important for us to exhibit kindness not just to those who have been kind to us?*

⌛ *What is vengeance?*

⌛ *Why do you believe vengeance belongs only to the Lord and not to us?*

Hope Is on the Way!

God knew Joseph would require divine intervention to walk out his destiny. And so our God, who "machashabs" what the enemy meant for evil into an extraordinary good, planned ahead of time for Joseph's deliverance from the pit.

> *Then they sat down to eat a meal. And as they raised their eyes and looked, behold,*
> *a caravan of Ishmaelites was coming from Gilead, with their camels bearing*
> *aromatic gum and balm and myrrh, on their way to bring them down to Egypt.*
> **(Genesis 37:25)**

I wonder when that caravan of Ishmaelites left from its starting point? I wonder if they were detained by a sandstorm, if a camel had a lame leg, or they were forced to rest for a day. I wonder.

At just the right moment, this caravan left from a certain geographical location, made just enough stops and encountered just enough bumps to pass through Dothan on just the right day at just the right time. This caravan had no idea that the purpose for their journey was not to deliver aromatic gum, balm, and myrrh to Egypt, but God had a purpose that trumped their economic venture. This caravan, from the beginning of time, possessed a primary purpose of delivering Joseph into his destiny. If God did that for Joseph, He will certainly do it for you as well.

⧖   *Are you encouraged yet? How is the story of Joseph raising your faith level?*

Prevenient Grace

There is an archaic theological phrase that few in the twenty-first century have thought to consider or are even aware of. It is the phrase "prevenient grace." John Wesley is attributed with conceiving this wonderful term that literally means "grace that goes before." Prevenient grace is the grace that precedes human action and powerfully reflects God's heart for His creation. The word *prevenient* comes from two Latin words, *pre* meaning "before" and *venio* meaning "to go." Thus, prevenient grace is grace that has gone before and prepared the way. The caravan was God's prevenient grace given to Joseph in his time of deep trouble.

> *But He gives a greater grace. Therefore it says, "God is opposed to the proud, but*
> *gives grace to the humble." (James 4:6)*

⧖   *Have you ever experienced prevenient grace in your life? How so?*

⧗   *How does James 4:6 tell the story of Joseph?*

God has seen ahead, down the hallways of your life, and knows exactly what you need. A caravan is on its way.

⧗   *What is your definition of the word grace?*

⧗   *Enjoy your treasure verse for the week. As you ponder it, make a list of all the promises hidden in this verse.*

God never said that the journey would be easy, but he did say that the arrival would be worthwhile.

—*Max Lucado*
Safe in the Shepherd's Arms

Day 4

How Mean Can You Be?!

I am absolutely amazed at the cruelty of human behavior at times. When I hear of a shooting at a mall or in a school, I weep with those who have been impacted. When I watch the nightly news and hear of the vicious behavior of certain governments and leaders, I shake my head in disbelief. When I am met with the reality of unprovoked persecution in daily life, I have no words to describe my soul's reaction. However, nothing disturbs me more deeply than when brutality takes place within the family unit—there is no heartbreak like family heartbreak.

> *Judah said to his brothers, "What profit is it for us to kill our brother and cover up his blood? Come and let us sell him to the Ishmaelites and not lay our hands on him, for he is our brother, our own flesh." And his brothers listened to him. Then some Midianite traders passed by, so they pulled him up and lifted Joseph out of the pit, and sold him to the Ishmaelites for twenty shekels of silver. Thus they brought Joseph into Egypt.*
>
> *Now Reuben returned to the pit, and behold, Joseph was not in the pit; so he tore his garments. He returned to his brothers and said, "The boy is not there; as for me, where am I to go?" So they took Joseph's tunic, and slaughtered a male goat and dipped the tunic in the blood; and they sent the varicolored tunic and brought it to their father and said, "We found this; please examine it to see whether it is your son's tunic or not." (Genesis 37:26–32)*

The traders in Genesis 37:25 and again in Genesis 37:28 are referenced by two different names: the Midianites and the Ishmaelites. These are merely two different names for the same group of people. *Ishmaelite* is likely the broad term while *Midianite* is the smaller, ethnic reference. These two people groups both descended from Abraham, both lived in the same region, and were associated in many ways. So, we see in Scripture an interchangeable use of their names.

The Injustice

Let's focus on the great injustice of this passage of Scripture. How mean can a group of young men actually be? They sold their little brother into slavery, ripped his valuable coat off his body, laced the coat with animal blood, and then lied to their father about it all. These are not a group of innocent Boy Scouts; they are a gang of hoodlums who are heartless and vicious. They represent a picture of humanity at its very worst.

The raging siblings sold Joseph for only twenty pieces of silver, which was the common rate for a slave. How could Joseph's brothers imagine that his life was only worth twenty pieces of silver? Whenever we, as the children of God, undervalue the life of another, we too, are guilty of selling them for mere silver. We must apply this great injustice to our personal appraisal when measuring the lives of others. How do you value the unborn? The unemployed? Those whose skin has more or less pigmentation than yours? Those in prison?

⏳   *How can you demonstrate the fact that you value the unborn?*

⏳   *How can you demonstrate the truth that you believe homeless people are of great worth?*

⏳   *How can you show that your heart esteems those whose skin may have a different hue than yours?*

Just as we are aghast at the treatment of Joseph by his brothers, we must also examine our own hearts and contemplate this question. *Who have I been guilty of selling for only twenty pieces of silver?* The words of Jesus echo through the canyons of time and land in our hearts today.

Then the righteous will answer Him, "Lord, when did
we see You hungry, and feed You, or thirsty, and give You something
to drink? And when did we see You a stranger,
and invite You in, or naked, and clothe You? When did
we see You sick, or in prison, and come to You?"
The King will answer and say to them, "Truly I say to you,
to the extent that you did it to one of these brothers of Mine,
even the least of them, you did it to Me."

—Matthew 25:37–40

Screaming Out in Pain

I can't help but wonder what happened in Joseph's mind and heart while this vivid and unbelievable action took place. I can only imagine that his emotions screamed out in pain, *God, where are You? Why am I here? Do You see me? Have you forsaken me? Will you please send someone to help me?*

The reason I know Joseph likely called out to the Lord in his moment of distress is that God did indeed hear Joseph, and He sent someone to help him.

My friend, no matter what you are going through today and regardless of how you have been mistreated, God is working behind the scenes of your life. There is something transpiring beyond what you can see with your human eyes. That "something" is the prevenient grace of God.

⧗   *What was the worst moment of your life?*

⧗   *What was going on in your heart and mind during that awful time?*

I am sure Joseph did not for one minute believe the caravan was God's answer for his life—but it was. What you see today with your natural eye may not *seem* to be your answer either, but you don't see what God sees. You don't know what God knows. You are oblivious to the potential for promise in your tawdry situation. Although you may not realize it, you have been divinely set up through your untoward circumstances for greatness and destiny.

⧗   *What does it mean to walk by faith and not by sight when you are going through a difficult period in life?*

⧗   *Spend some time memorizing the treasure verse for the week. You might want to share it with someone who is going through a difficult season.*

God will meet you where you are in order
to take you where He wants you to go.

— Tony Evans
CSB Tony Evans Study Bible

Day 5

The Meanwhile of the Sad Story

H ave you ever thought you might die of a broken heart? Have you ever supposed you might not take another breath or live another day due to the magnitude of your emotional pain? Anyone who has lived to the ripe old age of thirty knows what I am referencing. Your wound might have been conceived due to "the other woman" or because of betrayal by a close family member. Perhaps the excruciating moment of unspeakable pain was ushered into your life through infertility, a health crisis, or a tragic accident. For Jacob, it was the awful realization that something horrific had happened to his son, Joseph.

> *Then he examined it and said, "It is my son's tunic. A wild beast has devoured him; Joseph has surely been torn to pieces!" So Jacob tore his clothes, and put sackcloth on his loins and mourned for his son many days. Then all his sons and all his daughters arose to comfort him, but he refused to be comforted. And he said, "Surely I will go down to Sheol in mourning for my son." So his father wept for him.* (Genesis 37:33–35)

Jacob mourned for many days when he was confronted with the death of Joseph, his dearly loved son. If there is a pain greater than losing a child to early death, I don't know what it is. Jacob's grief was not just a knee-jerk reaction to circumstances he despised, he was engulfed in the white-hot, searing pain of agony. His lamentation was so great that he even thought he would die. I can hardly read the above verses without experiencing the enormity of the anguish of Jacob.

The structure of this dysfunctional family had been ripped apart, just as Joseph's coat had been torn asunder. Nothing would ever be the same for Jacob. Instead of twelve strapping sons, he now only had eleven living. Where Joseph used to sit at the family table, grief sat in his seat. Not only had Joseph's varicolored coat been destroyed but so had camaraderie, the joy of unity, and the power of hope. Was this the end of their story? Would this family shrivel up and die due to the grossly poor choices of the older brothers? What would happen now to the household of Jacob? Could they ever recover?

Just One Word

The very next verse in the story of Joseph is perhaps one of the most powerful Scriptures in the entire Old Testament. On this one verse hinges the power of God to turn bad into good, evil into benevolent, and loss into gain.

> *Meanwhile, the Midianites sold him in Egypt to Potiphar, Pharaoh's officer, the* *captain of the bodyguard.* **(Genesis 37:36)**

Meanwhile. When your world has fallen apart, never forget that there is a meanwhile. When all you see with your naked eye is death, remind yourself of the meanwhile. If your world has suddenly morphed into grief and the black pit, restore your soul with this one word—meanwhile.

When life has treated you unfairly there is a meanwhile going on behind the scenes of your life. God just may be taking the very worst moment of your life and using it as a transformational power to usher you into a divine promotion. God has the power and willingness to take a horrific situation and temper it with his meanwhile, producing something incredible beyond human understanding.

Joseph *could* have remained at home as a little shepherd boy taking care of his daddy and his brothers. He *could* have embraced the identity of a person with no eternal significance, and then you and I would never know his name. However, our God, who is a genius at everything, was able to take the injustice of this situation and turn it into a magnificent advantage, not only for Joseph, but for an entire nation. God used the cruel treatment of hard-hearted family members, added in His prevenient grace, and miraculously transformed it into history-shaping events.

Some of you reading this today may be going through a meanwhile time in your own life. I have found there are seasons when a meanwhile can be just what it says—a mighty *mean*-while. As God is working in the meanwhiles of life, the wait can feel vicious, agonizing, and cruel. But when we trust the kind heart of the Father and give Him the time to transform our meanwhile, He will write the end of our stories. I have heard it said that if your story is not good, then God is not finished with it yet. While you are in the meanwhile, stay filled with faith and look at the events of your life from a historical perspective.

Your meanwhile, just like Joseph's, is about to become a miracle.

⧗   *What is your definition of the word miracle?*

It's a Theme

The theme of suffering is predominant in the narrative of Joseph, unable to be ignored. And the story of Joseph is about to get worse before it gets better. Joseph was a righteous young man, tapped by God for greatness in His unshakable kingdom, and yet, still he suffered. Joseph was protected, even during days of suffering, by his stable faith and awareness of the presence of the Lord. Follow Joseph's example. As you go through devastating life events, continue to embrace relentless faith, and remind yourself daily that the Lord is with you. Our faithful God is able to create overpowering good out of suffering and evil—never doubt it.

⧗   *Can you think of someone else who suffered in Scripture for righteousness' sake?*

⧗   *How did you see the goodness of God intervene in their story?*

⧗   *How has memorizing the treasure verse this week encouraged your faith?*

Suffering is never for nothing.

—*Elisabeth Elliot*

THE JOSEPH PRINCIPLE

A Tale of Prevenient Grace

On July 20, 2012, a mass shooting occurred inside a movie theater in Aurora, Colorado, during a midnight screening of a newly released movie. Twelve people were killed, and seventy others were injured. At the time, the event marked the largest number of victims in one shooting in modern U.S. history.

One of those injured that fateful night was Petra Anderson, a gifted twenty-two-year-old composer and violinist. She was shot four times—three times in her arm and a fourth in her head. The fourth shot went in through Anderson's nose and rode up the back of her cranium. Instead of hitting her brain, however, the bullet traveled along a tiny extra tube of fluid. That defect, if you will, channeled the bullet away from inflicting severe brain injury.

Doctors initially feared the worst. They told Petra Anderson's family that if she lived, she could be paralyzed or have speech problems due to severe brain damage.

Remarkably, while removing the bullet from her brain and repairing the damage, doctors discovered a fluid-filled "void" she may have had since birth. Although these voids are not uncommon, the position of this particular cavity may have saved Petra's life.

A blog post, written by her family's pastor, described what happened.

> The shotgun buck shot . . . enters her brain from the exact point of this channel. The bullet is channeled from Petra's nose through her brain. It turns slightly, and comes to rest at the rear of her brain. And in the process, the bullet misses all the vital areas of the brain. All of them. In many ways, it almost *misses the brain* itself. . . . Like a giant BB through a straw created in Petra's brain before she was born, it follows the perfect route. The bullet moves in the least harmful way.[9]

According to Petra's sister, Chloe Anderson, the surgeon explained that this *channel* may have provided a kind of pathway for the piece of buck shot. It guided the invasive metal through Petra's brain, avoiding critical areas.

"If [the shot] had deviated, it could have hit major, major things," Chloe said. "It could have hit a blood vessel or her brain stem. I honestly don't know how it's possible for the bullet to travel so straight."

Whether it was a physical anomaly in Petra's brain or just the miracle path that the bullet traveled, this was highly unusual. Petra was the beneficiary of what John Wesley referred to as "prevenient grace." God prepared a way before she was shot in the head for the bullet to travel through her brain and make no lasting difference.

Petra is now married, and her wounds have healed. Her mind is clear, and she is playing her own music again. She is fully alive and says, "We will move forward with joy. God has done a wonderful thing in our lives."[10]

While it looks like things are out of control, behind the scenes there is a God who has not surrendered His authority.

—A. W. Tozer
God's Power for Your Life

Week 4

———

Meanwhiles
Become Miracles

Stuff

We have all gone through "stuff" we honestly did not enjoy and certainly would not have chosen if God had given us that choice. While traveling through those difficult places, we might wonder if God had forgotten us or if we had done something to deserve our pit of rotten circumstances. I imagine many of us have experienced absolute incredulity at the way people treated us and have cried out to God, "I don't like this! I don't like it one little bit!" We can all passionately admit that much of life is hard. Sometimes the stuff of life is simply exhausting and disgusting.

As we walk through the painful journey often required on this side of heaven, our soul adamantly refuses to remain satisfied with pain, disappointment, and mistreatment. However, when we look at the hard stuff through eyes of faith based upon the Word of God, we can all be assured that He is able to transform our horrible stuff into something that smacks of heaven's goodness. It's what God does best. The Lord takes untold delight in turning what was once painful into something valuable beyond measure. Only God.

⧗   *This is a difficult question and will likely require thought, prayer, and deep conversations with those you trust in their faith walk. Do you believe God causes hard things to happen to His children?*

⧗   *Or do you believe God allows hard things to happen to His children?*

An Expert

When I look at the engine of a car, all I see is dirt, grease, and metal. I see nothing pretty or valuable under the hood. However, when a mechanic examines my engine, he or she can see the carburetor purring with the alternator and discern if it has enough oil, water, and energy. How is a mechanic able to do this? They have studied the book. They know the purpose of each sustaining part.

When I look at an algebraic equation, I am nearly blinded by the mass of numbers staring back at my vapidly confused face. In addition to the puzzle of numerical symbols that are dancing in front of my eyes, letters, variables, and exponents are added to the three-ring circus. I see no way out of the riddle presented to me. I struggle in total confusion and the chaos of too much information. However, when a mathematician looks at the very same equation, he or she views pure joy. They quickly discover an answer or a solution to the mathematical problem. How is a mathematician able to accomplish this impossible feat? It's because he or she has studied the math textbook and they know how to navigate their way through a series of numerical acrobatics.

I was a homeschool mom for nearly twenty-five years and by the time my third son studied biology, you would have thought I mastered it. But when the dissection kit arrived, complete with a worm, fish, and frog, I didn't have a clue what to do or how to identify the inner body parts. I can't tell a kidney from a liver from a heart. Who do you think I am? Einstein? You've got to be kidding me!

All I saw was mush, yuck, and piles of gross innards. But a biologist looks inside a specimen and quickly identifies a well-ordered system of divinely designed organs. Why? Because the biologist has studied the biology book and he or she knows how systems work and where they have been placed in the body of an animal or human being. The biologist reverts to what he or she has studied.

⌛ *What subjects have you studied? Are you an expert in anything?*

⌛ *How have you become knowledgeable in a certain field? Through education? Reading or self-taught? Life experiences?*

Why Read?

This is exactly why we study the Bible, my friends. We study so when life happens, and we don't like what we see with our natural eyes and are forced to deal with situations we don't understand, we have wisdom. We can revert to what we learned from the Word. We are experts in our field of study because we have consistently read and digested the Book. The Bible guarantees that between its two covers, you will discover jam-packed content filled with hope, practical knowledge, divine revelation, and wisdom. When a common man or an ordinary woman studies the Bible, it enables them to overcome any situation encountered in life.

We are examining the story of Joseph as found in the book of Genesis to help us with the devastation we often tackle in our human circumstances. We will all encounter a Joseph moment or two, when our world has collapsed around us. By delving into the Bible, we will have the tools we need to walk through the pain with an extraordinary purpose and an awareness of the goodness of God.

⌛ *How much time do you spend daily in the Word of God? Is it hit or miss or is it consistent?*

⌛ *Do you use a particular plan when you read the Bible, or do you just choose a random passage?*

⌛ *How do you feel you could improve the time you spend reading the Bible?*

Let's Review

After Joseph's brothers ripped his coat off him, threw him into the pit, sold him to a caravan of traders, and dripped blood on his coat, they cruelly convinced their father, Jacob, that Joseph was dead. Jacob pictured his dear son being torn limb from limb and mutilated by a fierce animal due to the condition of his coat. Jacob mourned Joseph's death for days.

Then he examined it and said, "It is my son's tunic. A wild beast has devoured him; Joseph has surely been torn to pieces!" So Jacob tore his clothes, and put sackcloth on his loins and mourned for his son many days. Then all his sons and all his daughters arose to comfort him, but he refused to be comforted. And he said, "Surely I will go down to Sheol in mourning for my son." So his father wept for him. (Genesis 37:33–35)

The Ishmaelites or Midianites sold Joseph to Potiphar, an Egyptian officer of Pharaoh. The Midianites knew they had happened upon treasure in the flesh—Joseph was young, good-looking, and strong. Likely, these savvy traders checked Joseph's teeth and felt his muscles as they pondered the price the brothers were expecting to get for their very own blood relative. Joseph was the whole package, and the Midianites sealed the deal.

The meanwhile in Joseph's life had begun.

Meanwhile, the Midianites sold him in Egypt to Potiphar, Pharaoh's officer, the captain of the bodyguard. (Genesis 37:36)

Hidden Treasure: Read this verse out loud several times today and write it out on a 3x5 card. Think about this verse throughout the week and begin to commit it to memory:

The Lord is the one who goes ahead of you; He will be with you. He will not fail you or forsake you. Do not fear or be dismayed.

—Deuteronomy 31:8

This is our time on the history line of God. This is it. What will we do with the one deep exhale of God on this earth? For we are but a vapor and we have to make it count. We're on. Direct us, Lord, and get us on our feet.

—Beth Moore

Day 2

Joseph Being Joseph

One of the most powerful yet ignored truths of our Christian faith is that the Lord is with us. He is always with us. He has promised never to leave us or forsake us no matter what we have done, how others have treated us, or what our living conditions may be like. The Lord is with you—just as He was with Joseph.

Circumstances can rip away our health, deprive us of finances, and mutilate relationships, but adverse conditions are unable to take the Lord's presence from us. Events may alienate us from family and situations may deny us of personal comfort, but they are unable to deprive us of the presence of the Lord. Joy, grace, and hope can never be deducted from a believer in Christ.

> *Now Joseph had been taken down to Egypt; and Potiphar, an Egyptian officer of Pharaoh, the captain of the bodyguard, bought him from the Ishmaelites, who had taken him down there. The Lord was with Joseph, so he became a successful man. And he was in the house of his master, the Egyptian.* **(Genesis 39:1–2)**

⧗ *What do you believe the most important phrase is in the above description of Joseph's new life?*

> *Now his master saw that the Lord was with him and how the Lord caused all that he did to prosper in his hand.* **(Genesis 39:3)**

⧗ *What do you believe is the most important phrase in the above verse?*

Well, by now you probably realize that the most important phrase in those two portions of Scripture is, *"The Lord was with Joseph."* It's breathtaking to me and unspeakably encouraging to know that even in slavery the Lord was with the young man, Joseph. The Holy Spirit, through the pen of Moses, gave us this sterling and powerful piece of information that should usher new hope into our lives today. *"The Lord was with Joseph."*

Don't Trust Your Heart

Do you recall our very first "Hidden Treasure" scripture?

For whatever was written in earlier times was written for our instruction, so that through perseverance and the encouragement of the Scriptures we might have hope.

—Romans 15:4

The phrase, *"The Lord was with Joseph,"* is written on the sacred pages of Scripture so you can live a life of hope. When your world comes crashing down around you, you can anticipate the goodness of God to invade your circumstances, because the Lord is with you. You can hold onto unwavering hope in all the meanwhile seasons simply because you are not alone. The Lord is with you. You are not forgotten. The trustworthy fact that the Lord is with you, just as He was with Joseph, changes everything for you. *The Lord is with you.* What wonderful and encouraging instruction we discover in these five astonishing words. *The Lord is with you.* His presence will enable us to persevere in all of life's challenges.

The heart is more deceitful than all else. (Jeremiah 17:9)

When we feel all dried up due to human pain and horrific circumstances, we must lean into our faith and not allow emotions to dictate our stability or level of hope. We must always remind ourselves of the eternal truth found in the Bible. We must also remind ourselves that our heart does not always tell the truth. Imagine that.

⧗   *How has your heart lied to you in the past?*

⧗ *What can you do, in a practical sense, to overcome the untruths your emotions might tell you?*

Blessing and Favor

In ancient Egypt, Potiphar didn't worry about paying the bills, taking out the trash, mowing the lawn, or picking up his kids from school. He didn't have to give thought to polishing the statues, overseeing the servants, or keeping the pantry well-stocked. Why? Because the stable and dependable Joseph was in charge. In Joseph, Potiphar had found a servant in whom he could depend.

This is a staggering detail so don't miss it. Joseph was a mere slave put in charge of everything in the home of one of the highest-ranking officials in all of Egypt. A slave in charge? Why, it's nearly an oxymoron.

> *So Joseph found favor in his sight and became his personal servant; and he made him overseer over his house, and all that he owned he put in his charge. It came about that from the time he made him overseer in his house and over all that he owned, the LORD blessed the Egyptian's house on account of Joseph; thus the LORD's blessing was upon all that he owned, in the house and in the field. So he left everything he owned in Joseph's charge; and with him there he did not concern himself with anything except the food which he ate. Now Joseph was handsome in form and appearance.* (Genesis 39:4–6)

⧗ *What do you believe are the two most important phrases in the above portion of Scripture? They are very similar.*

The honor Joseph earned just by being Joseph is astronomical. The blessing Joseph brought just by being Joseph is gargantuan. When a man or a woman chooses to live a life of integrity, honor, and righteousness, the results will also prove staggering.

⧗   *Who is the most honorable and righteous person you know?*

⧗   *Do you see an unmatched blessing upon his or her life?*

Father Abraham

When God spoke to Abraham, Joseph's great-grandfather, He made a promise to him and to his family:

> **And I will bless those who bless you,**
> **And the one who curses you I will curse.**
> **And in you all the families of the earth will be blessed.**
> **(Genesis 12:3)**

Joseph was decidedly becoming the walking-talking-living-breathing demonstration of the promise God declared decades prior. Joseph realized his purpose in life was to bless every single person in his world—whether they treated him well or not. I believe Joseph's purpose is not a singular one, but it is a call to all of us who are known as the children of God.

- If you are in a stressful situation at work—be a blessing.
- If you are dealing with a difficult person in your family—be a blessing.
- If you go into the grocery store—be a blessing.
- When you are at church—be a blessing.

Just as Joseph was Potiphar's ticket to blessing, you, as a woman of God, are the world's access to His blessings. When you walk into a room or into a relationship, you bring with you joy, hope, peace, and faith. Potiphar's family was heathen and did not know the God of the Bible, but they were blessed just because of one godly servant boy.

When a man or woman partners with God throughout even the most ravaging days of life, their imprint will last for generations to come. The Lord will turn slavery into leadership and rejection into the petri dish of miracles. Although Joseph was sold from an easy life of favoritism and coddling to the harshness of foreign bondage, he remained a man of honor and experienced the blessing of God.

⧖   *How does knowing "you are the world's access to the blessings of God" change your perspective on difficult situations?*

⧖   *How does knowing "you are the world's access to the blessings of God" change your perspective on difficult relationships?*

⧖   *Do something today to be a blessing to someone whom you encounter.*

⧖   *As we continue to review the story of Genesis, I want you to underline or circle in your Bible every time you read the phrase, "The Lord was with Joseph."*

⧖   *Be sure and take some time to study the treasure verse for the week. I always like to read a passage in different translations so I can understand its meaning.*

We are all faced with a series of great opportunities brilliantly disguised as impossible situations.

—Chuck Swindoll
The Swindoll Study Bible NLT

Day 3

True Character

The most difficult and horrific of days can show one's true character with much more clarity than is revealed during the gentle, delightful seasons of life. I believe anyone can reflect a person of honor and excellence when the sun is shining, the bills are paid, the grass is green, and the children are behaving well. However, when mean people invade our calm existence, when tragedy rears its unwelcome head, and when stress is a constant companion, our true character is revealed.

⏳ *Think of the last time your life was difficult—how did you treat people?*

⏳ *When stress shows up at the door of your heart, how do you respond?*

The Moment It Matters

Many people panic and refuse to tithe when finances are tight. Some folks resort to gossip and ill-treatment when others have been mean or fractious. However, in life's excruciatingly harsh days our character must reflect the character of the Lord.

Joseph could have chosen bitterness, anger, and depression—he certainly had the right to exhibit some of those emotions. However, he chose not to do so. Even though his story was one of *"from riches to rags,"* Joseph chose the healthiest alternative as he determined to represent the Lord with excellence and honor. Joseph resolved that no matter where he was—home being cared for by his doting daddy or in the servant's quarters at Potiphar's house—he would tap into the wisdom of God. He embraced gracious heart attitudes and served those around him.

Joseph made Potiphar look good. Reflecting on Joseph's character during long days of loneliness, unresolved family issues, and detoured destiny has challenged me in my walk with the Father. I too, must make others' lives easier, even when my world has been rocked with disappointment and unfair treatment.

This philosophy I've lovingly named "The Joseph Principle" is for the workplace, home, and the church. When someone at work is harsh and unforgiving, demonstrate "The Joseph Principle." When someone in your family is not treating you kindly or honestly, apply "The Joseph Principle." When a person at church is cool towards you or obnoxious, lovingly manifest "The Joseph Principle."

⧖   *In your own words, write your version of what you believe "The Joseph Principle" means.*

Don't Ignore This

Joseph learned a lesson I often ignore—life is not about me. Life is not about my desire to be coddled and cared for. My life is about becoming a woman of excellence and exhibiting the character traits of honor, integrity, and wisdom. I was created in the image of God to demonstrate His character and then to enthusiastically serve others, no matter who the others might be. I must be gentle, truthful, and loving with obnoxious in-laws, a mean boss, and a neighbor who won't leave me alone. It's why I am here—to be a vibrant show and tell of "The Joseph Principle."

> *Now his master saw that the Lord was with him and how the Lord caused all that he did to prosper in his hand.*
>
> *It came about that from the time he made him overseer in his house and over all that he owned, the Lord blessed the Egyptian's house on account of Joseph; thus the Lord's blessing was upon all that he owned, in the house and in the field.* **(Genesis 39:3, 5)**

⧖   *Who is most difficult for you to be kind and gentle toward? Take some time to pray for this person today and ask God to help you.*

Thousands of Years Later

About two thousand years after Joseph spent time as a slave in Potiphar's home, an extraordinary man by the name of Stephen was called upon to defend his faith in Christ before the Jewish council. As Stephen recounted all God had done for His people in earlier years, this is what Stephen said of Joseph,

---

The patriarchs became jealous of Joseph and sold him into Egypt.
Yet God was with him.

— Acts 7:9

This is the legacy of the entitled son, who was thrown into a pit, sold into slavery, and who ultimately served those around him. "Yet God was with him." God was with the man-child Joseph, despite horrendous events. How wonderful to know the God of Joseph is with you as well. Don't be captured by your troubles but commit to a triumphant walk through your trials. Declare that your eyes are fixed upon the Lord, not fixated on what you are going through so painfully. From the life of Joseph and testimony of Stephen, we can stand assured that it is within our power to choose our own legacy.

How will you be remembered? As a woman who spoke her own mind and spewed verbal vomit on everyone within hearing distance? When your family talks about you forty to fifty years from now, will they sadly shake their heads as they remember a woman who worried her way through life? Or will they remember you just like Joseph was remembered? "Her life may not have been perfect, but the Lord was with her everywhere she went."

⧖   *What is the legacy you hope to leave?*

⧖   *Don't forget to mark the phrase "The Lord was with Joseph" every time you see it in the narrative.*

⏳ *Underline the meaningful words in the treasure verse and spend some time meditating on them.*

We can see hope in the midst of hopelessness. We can see peace in the midst of chaos. We have a hope that the world does not have. We can see clearly that all things work together for the good of them that love Him and are called according to His purpose.

—Priscilla Shirer

Day 4

Joseph and the Horrible, No-Good, Very Bad Day

Joseph is about to experience a horrible, no-good, very bad day. You and I will be the beneficiaries of the lessons Joseph's situation teaches about these kinds of awful, rotten occurrences. We will observe the miraculous possibility of living *above* your circumstances even while you are *in* your circumstances. From the life of Joseph, we will ascertain the potential to remain faithful to God in the midst of a rotten day.

⧖ *How should we respond emotionally to a difficult day?*

⧖ *How should we respond spiritually to a difficult day?*

Easy On the Eyes

The Bible gives interesting specifics concerning Joseph's appearance. I am always amazed by some of the details I find, and this is one of those places where I grin and remark, *Holy Spirit, thank You for including that tidbit of information. You didn't have to do it, but I am so glad You did.*

Now Joseph was handsome in form and appearance. (Genesis 39:6)

⧗   *Why do you think the Holy Spirit included this detail about Joseph's appearance?*

Joseph was not only a fine-looking young man, but he also had the body of an athlete. I imagine the young servant girls in the home of Pharaoh had their eyes on him. Perhaps they giggled every time Joseph walked by. But Joseph's good looks weren't enough to protect him from harsh experiences in life. As a matter of fact, in the upcoming scene, Joseph's attractive face and well-honed body only exacerbated his very bad day.

Yet Another Test

Satan tempted Joseph with unfair treatment and then with the loss of his destiny and family relationships. Joseph's next fierce battle took place when he was a slave. In all these events, Joseph overcame. He thrived in the face of pain, and he held the sweet understanding of God with him. However, Joseph was met with yet another battle.

> *It came about after these events that his master's wife looked with desire at Joseph, and she said, "Lie with me." But he refused and said to his master's wife, "Behold, with me here, my master does not concern himself with anything in the house, and he has put all that he owns in my charge. There is no one greater in this house than I, and he has withheld nothing from me except you, because you are his wife. How then could I do this great evil and sin against God? (Genesis 39:7–9)*

Joseph was tempted by a woman. Pharaoh's wife was a seductress and attempted to flirt her way into Joseph's arms. If she had her way with Joseph, he would commit physical sin with the wife of his master. Such a thought was abominable to the young, handsome Joseph.

Joseph thus far in the narrative has not given in to despair or bad attitudes, but the question lingers, will he give in to moral compromise? From Scripture, we know Joseph understood that being in a sexual relationship with Potiphar's wife was not only a betrayal of human trust, but it was a sin against God. Joseph might have been young but his wisdom echoes through the ages and settles into my heart. I know when I sin, my chief betrayal is against the Lord whom I love dearly.

This is a powerful and intimate lesson for all of us. When you are tempted to sin, remember that not only are you betraying yourself, but you are also betraying God. My heart breaks as I recall the moments and times when I chose to sin and therefore disappointed the One who cares the most about me and who loves me unconditionally. Why would I sin against the One who has my name engraved on His hands?

⌛ *Does a sin haunt you? Perhaps you should take the time to repent right now and ask for the Father's forgiveness.*

Day After Day

Pharaoh's wife was relentless and every day she begged Joseph to partner with her in sexual sin. I wonder how she did it, don't you? Now, because I know feminine nature and how cunning women can be, I imagine she dressed in her most provocative clothes and purred softly to the young, righteous man. I wonder if she used perfume and oils to make herself seem more comely and desirable.

> **As she spoke to Joseph day after day, he did not listen to her to lie beside her or be with her. (Genesis 39:10)**

Joseph ignored this paramour and refused to give in to her enticement. Once again, Joseph passed the test set before him.

Sin is much like Pharaoh's relentless wife. Sin will try to chase you down, dress itself up, and make itself smell good. Even with the charming pretense that sin inevitably offers, it is still ugly. Sin is deceptive and will try to cover itself up in cultural acceptance or in emotional justification. Don't believe the wiles of sin! Wrap yourself up in the sweet knowledge that God is with you even on your worst day. Remind yourself often that when you sin, it is God you are disappointing with your compromising actions.

As I travel through life and make it a high priority to live above reproach, I often think of this New Testament scripture:

Abstain from all appearance of evil.

—1 Thessalonians 5:22 KJV

The Bible, in its infinite wisdom, gives life-changing advice in this very short but complete verse. If a situation smells like sin—run away. If an action looks questionable—run away. If even a word is tainted with moral compromise—don't say it. In our minds, we tend to justify so many of our actions and words and use our culture as the litmus test. But, my sisters, it is this simple—if the Bible says, "No," then don't do it.

⧖   *Take some time to ponder the magnificence of our treasure verse this week. What does it mean that God is with you on your worst day?*

*God will not permit any troubles to come upon us, unless
He has a specific plan by which great blessing
can come out of the difficulty.*

— Peter Marshall

Day 5

An Excruciating Lesson

Joseph will learn an excruciating lesson through this experience with Pharaoh's flirtatious wife. We also need to learn the lesson of Joseph on this day—never place yourself in a situation where moral compromise could potentially happen. Joseph, thus far, has proven to be a young man of valor and honor. We must applaud him for keeping a pure heart and for tenaciously hanging onto the presence of God. However, if Joseph made a mistake, perhaps we are about to encounter it.

> **Now it happened one day that Joseph went into the house to do his work, and none of the men of the household was there inside. (Genesis 39:11)**

Joseph, perhaps naively, went into Pharaoh's home when none of the other male servants were inside to serve as chaperones or protectors from the loose woman. His innocent mistake would eventually impact at least the next two years of Joseph's life. Although we cannot blame Joseph and accuse him of verifiable sin in this situation, it is true that our actions have long-term consequences.

⧗ *Have you ever had a moment when, although you did not sin, you know you made an error in judgment? What could you have done differently?*

⧗ *Is there a difference between "making a mistake" and sinning?*

Run, Joseph! Run!

Joseph was still a young man when these events transpired but he was about to learn that age-old lesson and find himself in some extra-hot trouble. Hell definitely hath no fury like a woman scorned.

> *She caught Joseph by his garment, saying, "Lie with me!" And he left his garment in her hand and fled, and went outside.* (Genesis 39:12)

My friend, when sin reaches for you . . . run! Run as hard and as fast as you can in the opposite direction of sin. Don't hesitate. Don't flirt with sin. Don't play with sin. Don't reason with sin because sin is unreasonable. Joseph ran and so should you. Don't enter an alliance with sin but ignore it and escape it as quickly as you can.

Be of sober spirit, be on the alert. Your adversary, the devil, prowls around like a roaring lion, seeking someone to devour. But resist him, firm in your faith, knowing that the same experiences of suffering are being accomplished by your brethren who are in the world.

—1 Peter 5:8–9

Joseph's garment, once again, will cause Joseph some devastating trouble and long-lasting anguish. Last time he landed in the pit because of his garment and this time he will land in prison.

⧗   *What do you believe Joseph's garment represents in this part of the story?*

Falsely Accused

Joseph, even as a young man, refused to give in to temporary pleasures in exchange for God's eternal blessing. Even when you have done the right thing and have refused to do the wrong thing, you might be falsely accused. Even when you have run the other way quickly, you might still be falsely accused. It is not an uncommon thing for the best of God's children to face fabrications of the worst of sins.

When she saw that he had left his garment in her hand and had fled outside, she called to the men of her household and said to them, "See, he has brought in a Hebrew to us to make sport of us; he came in to me to lie with me, and I screamed. When he heard that I raised my voice and screamed, he left his garment beside me and fled and went outside." So she left his garment beside her until his master came home. Then she spoke to him with these words, "The Hebrew slave, whom you brought to us, came in to me to make sport of me; and as I raised my voice and screamed, he left his garment beside me and fled outside." **(Genesis 39:13–18)**

Sin is ugly, evil, and deceptive and there will be moments in life when, like Joseph, the enemy will try to falsely accuse you of giving in to sin. Jesus was falsely accused, and we can expect to be treated just like Him.

⧗   *Have you ever been falsely accused?*

⧗   *Have you ever been the victim of gossip? How did that make you feel?*

⧗   *What is it in a person that would provoke him or her to fabricate a lie against someone?*

What Would Jesus Do?

Perhaps we would all benefit from pausing in the story of Joseph. Let's look at scriptures that enable us to live a life of sterling faith, even when we have been falsely accused of sin or moral compromise. Let's lean in and listen to a situation that Jesus found Himself in as He was brought before Pilate.

Early in the morning the chief priests with the elders and scribes and the whole Council, immediately held a consultation; and binding Jesus, they led Him away and delivered Him to Pilate. Pilate questioned Him, "Are You the King of the Jews?" And He answered him, "It is as you say." The chief priests began to accuse Him harshly. Then Pilate questioned Him again, saying, "Do You not answer? See how many charges they bring against You!" But Jesus made no further answer; so Pilate was amazed.

—Mark 15:1–5

Jesus didn't defend Himself—how amazing is that? If anyone was guilt-free and had the right of self-defense it was Jesus. But He didn't choose denial. He trusted His Father to be His strong Defender in front of Pilate.

Years ago, when my husband Craig was pastoring a large church, some unfair and untrue accusations were made against us. We determined to hold onto our joy, walk in victory, and not defend ourselves. Many people told us later that our refusal to discuss the situation and thereby slander anyone else convinced them of our honor.

If you have been falsely accused, remember who the accuser of the brethren is (Revelation 12:10). Accusations that try to assassinate your character are actually from the pit of hell. You can be assured that it is not a person, but Satan, trying to steal your joy and usher depression into your life.

What a victorious strategy to keep our eyes on Jesus and not on human beings when we have been vilified. Do not be deceived, no person or group of people are attempting to malign your character—it is the enemy himself. Your winning strategy is to forgive people, bind the devil, and keep your heart set on Jesus Christ.

When Craig and I were enduring that horrible church situation, we also decided to bless those who were mistreating us. We made it a high and intentional priority to say kind things about our accusers and to lift them up in the eyes of others. God's ideas are best and I must obey His Word even when I would rather flaunt my emotions.

Blessed are you when people insult you and persecute you, and falsely say all kinds of evil against you because of Me. Rejoice and be glad, for your reward in heaven is great; for in the same way they persecuted the prophets who were before you.

—Matthew 5:11–12

The Bible actually works, my friends. When you bless others, you yourself will receive a blessing in return.

⏳ *Write out the four principles you can stand on when you have been falsely accused, given in these verses:*

1. _____

2. _____

3. _____

4. _____

The Most Amazing Thing

Once again, the Lord was with Joseph just as He is with you. The Lord was with Joseph and extended kindness and favor to him even when he was unfairly thrown into prison.

> *Now when his master heard the words of his wife, which she spoke to him, saying, "This is what your slave did to me," his anger burned. So Joseph's master took him and put him into the jail, the place where the king's prisoners were confined; and he was there in the jail. But the Lord was with Joseph and extended kindness to him, and gave him favor in the sight of the chief jailer. The chief jailer committed to Joseph's charge all the prisoners who were in the jail; so that whatever was done there, he was responsible for it. (Genesis 39:19–22)*

Don't miss this. The Lord was with Joseph just as He is with you. The Lord extended kindness and favor to him even when he was unfairly thrown into prison. How wonderful to remember that when we are in the worst place imaginable, God has not changed. His presence remains and His character is constant. He is still a God of eternal goodness and unending kindness. He showers all that He is and all He has upon His children. Dreadful events may deny outward blessings and confine us in a dungeon of pain, but they are unable to deprive us of sweet communion with God, our Father and Creator.

Favor is an undeserved gift that comes from God, not from mankind. If you are experiencing devastation today, spend some time in prayer and ask God for the same favor that was given to Joseph. Favor is heaven's lovely idea expressly given toward a man or a woman in pain.

⏳ *What is your definition of the word favor?*

⧖   *Who has shown kindness to you when you have been in a difficult situation? How did that make you feel?*

The Stuff of Which Heroes Are Made

"You can't keep a good man down." In those seven words so often quoted, we read the story of Joseph. I can't help but wonder what type of mettle Joseph was made from. I want that same mettle.

> **The chief jailer did not supervise anything under Joseph's charge because the Lord was with him; and whatever he did, the Lord made to prosper. (Genesis 39:23)**

Joseph's emotional constitution was exceptionally stellar. In him, we see a young man made of the stuff of which heroes are made.

The sterling truth is that you are made of that same stuff. Your only requirement is a willing heart and a commitment to integrity and excellence. If you long to walk in the favor and blessing that Joseph experienced, then you, too, must embrace an attitude that shouts loudly, "God is in charge. I will not be shaken!"

It was the Lord who enabled Joseph to prosper at home with his daddy, to be blessed in Potiphar's house, and to stand as a leader even in prison. It is the Lord who can cause you to prosper as well.

If you are on a fixed income, continue to live a life of honor and financial integrity and just see what God will do for you. When you are a giver, your income has the potential for multiplication. If you need a new job, keep serving with excellence and faithfulness at your current position and expect God to open doors for you. If you deeply desire children and haven't been able to conceive, volunteer to work in the church nursery or to teach Sunday School. If you long for marriage and are praying for a man of God to come into your life, take a widow out to dinner or volunteer to babysit for a large family, so the parents can go on a date.

⧖   *What are some of the attributes you highly respect in a person who might be a hero or a heroine to you?*

Believers have no control over every life experience; however, we can respond to unjust circumstances with faith and integrity. The person who is faithful in the small things in life will ultimately be responsible for greater things.

> *His master said to him, "Well done, good and faithful slave.*
> *You were faithful with a few things, I will put you in charge*
> *of many things; enter into the joy of your master."*
>
> *—Matthew 25:21*

At the lowest point in Joseph's life, in the strangeness of a foreign land, with no friend and no prospect for release, God initiated the steps that brought about deliverance for Joseph, his family, and the world. What miracles might God produce from your situation?

⧗ *For one last time, enjoy this week's treasure verse. Share it with someone and remind this person of God's presence in their life as well.*

> *However many blessings we expect from God,*
> *His infinite liberality will always exceed all*
> *our wishes and our thoughts.*
>
> *—John Calvin*

THE JOSEPH PRINCIPLE

Corrie ten Boom

There is an extraordinary historical account of a woman who was overweight her entire adult life and never married. Yet, she longed for a home, a husband, and children of her own. She lived with her parents and older sister while working in the family business.

The one bright spot in an otherwise mundane week came when she taught the special needs Sunday school class at church. Although this spinster never gave birth to children of her own, she delighted in teaching little ones who struggled to sit still and would never be accepted into a university. She taught children with Down syndrome how to worship like David with their hands high in the air, dancing erratically around the cramped Sunday school classroom. They sang off-key at the top of their small, but very loud, lungs.

This enthusiastic teacher taught the children how to be brave like Daniel and to look for angels rather than at lions.

The Dutch heroine, Corrie, taught these sweet little minds and hearts that God always takes care of His children. And like Moses, when others are unkind to God's people, God will lead them into His promised land.

This courageous middle-aged woman of the twentieth century found delight in entertaining missionaries and other friends from church in her parents' simple home. They often enjoyed a meal and then entered into a raucous evening of games followed by a reverent time of singing hymns and reading the Bible together.

Although never a mother, this woman had deep maternal longings. Her favorite person was her nephew, Peter, named after the bold fisherman who loved Jesus without reserve.

Whenever she battled loneliness, she offered to babysit one of the children in her Sunday school class, so the tired parents could have a well-deserved night off.

In spite of her weight, marital status, and never traveling outside of her own village, this woman lived vibrantly with her elderly parents until in her mid-fifties. But she still discovered the secret of abundant life at its finest. She embraced what she had been given and turned it into a valuable and breathtaking masterpiece of living.

Eventually, the dear, special-needs children, whom Corrie loved ferociously, began to disappear out of her weekly Sunday school class. One by one they ceased to show up for their favorite hour of the week. They were being taken from their parents and placed in state institutions by the government. Corrie's heart was broken, not only for herself, but also for the distraught and helpless families.

Shortly after the children began to disappear, Corrie's father gathered their family around the table and informed them that the ten Boom family would be making some serious changes. They would build a hidden room upstairs in their home and welcome visitors who would live in this hiding place. The ten Boom family was a Christian family of conviction and honor and were joining the ranks of hundreds of others who were assisting the Jews. Holland's Jews were being sent to concentrations camps under one of the most evil regimes of all time.

By the end of World War II, this one family, the ten Booms, had saved over eight hundred Jews, as well as hundreds of Dutch underground workers.

On February 28, 1944, the Gestapo arrived and took six members of Corrie's family to prison. Although the violent Nazis ransacked the entire home and systematically searched everywhere, they never found the secret room where six Jews remained in hiding. These Jews were rescued by the Dutch Resistance nearly forty-seven hours later.

Everyone in Corrie's family, except Corrie herself, died in concentration camps. She was the sole ten Boom survivor of this horrific injustice, when she arrived home alone to live again. Thus began Corrie's lifelong ministry around the world. Corrie testified everywhere she traveled, making statements like these:

"There is no pit that God is not deeper still."

"God gives us the love to forgive our enemies."

"Jesus always wins the final victory!"[11]

Corrie ten Boom tramped for the Lord for thirty-three years, until she was eighty-eight years old. She only retired after a stroke that took her speech.

Although Corrie was not Jewish by birth, she protected and cared for the ancient people of God. The Jews have a long-held belief that only truly blessed people die on the day of their birth. Corrie walked into eternity on her ninety-first birthday, April 15, 1983.

Corrie knew how to embrace the abundant life Jesus promised, even while in a cruel prison of man's making. She could have been a depressed, lonely woman lacking any true purpose in life. Instead, Corrie gave all she had to give, loved when others hated, and poured herself out in Christ's name, to the children under her charge and a war-torn world.

Don't bother to give God instructions;
just report for duty.

—*Corrie ten Boom*

Week 5

A Royal Mess

Day 1

Sweet, Sweet Surrender

Have you ever wondered how God could possibly use someone like you? If you have asked yourself—and God—that question, you are in good company. Broken people are the only type of people God ever uses. Messed up folks with a checkered past are His grand specialty.

The Lord can take the greatest tragedy of your life and turn it into a moment of unmatched triumph. How does that happen? When does this happen?

When we surrender and relinquish our pain for His sweet peace, exchanging our opinions for His wise authority, a miracle happens. Regardless of what takes place in our circumstances, a wonder always emerges from the deepest part of our souls.

⧗ *What does it mean to surrender to the Lord?*

⧗ *Is there something or someone you need to surrender to the Lord today?*

In the Dungeon

Joseph chose a personal surrender to God's ways and His eternal wisdom while he spent time in an undeserved prison experience. It's time to travel to the Egyptian dungeon and join Joseph and his fellow prisoners. We'll learn what happens next in this riveting story.

Joseph shared a cell with two men who formerly served the king in the culinary division. Their once-favored positions had been ripped from them, and now they were prison-dwellers. How wonderful to note that our place in God's favor will never be taken from us—no matter how things look on the surface.

Then it came about after these things, the cupbearer and the baker for the king of Egypt offended their lord, the king of Egypt. Pharaoh was furious with his two officials, the chief cupbearer and the chief baker. So he put them in confinement in the house of the captain of the bodyguard, in the jail, the same place where Joseph was imprisoned. The captain of the bodyguard put Joseph in charge of them, and he took care of them; and they were in confinement for some time. (**Genesis 40:1–4**)

The cupbearer was on the royal staff of Pharaoh to taste the wine first, ensuring the king would not be poisoned by the drink. Similarly, the baker made sure the food of Pharaoh was in no way tainted so as to injure or even kill the king. In some manner, Scripture doesn't say exactly how, but both the cupbearer and baker offended Pharaoh.

Some biblical historians believe a type of poison was discovered in either Pharaoh's food or drink; therefore, both were placed under suspicion. You can understand why the king was furious if this indeed was the case. Both men were thrown into the same jail where Joseph was housed. They were likely cellmates with Joseph, although he was in charge of them. He took care of them for an undisclosed period of time.

Then the cupbearer and the baker for the king of Egypt, who were confined in jail, both had a dream the same night, each man with his own dream and each dream with its own interpretation. (**Genesis 40:5**)

When the cupbearer and baker had both been in prison for some time, they each had a dream on the very same night. Their dreams were unique and therefore the interpretation of the dreams required distinctive analysis.

⧗   *Has God ever spoken to you through a dream?*

⧗   *I find it valuable to keep a journal beside my bed so that when I do have a dream with perhaps some God-breathed significance, I am able to quickly write it out.*

The Mirror

The baker and cupbearer were apparently out of sorts one morning when Joseph went in to check on them. Joseph asked these two men why they were sad.

> *When Joseph came to them in the morning and observed them, behold, they were dejected. He asked Pharaoh's officials who were with him in confinement in his master's house, "Why are your faces so sad today?"* (Genesis 40:6–7)

Every time I read these two verses in the heart of Joseph's story I shake my head. I'd like to say to him, "Joseph, in case you haven't noticed, these two men are in prison. Isn't that enough reason to feel just a little down in the dumps? I might not be smiling either if I was in an Egyptian prison cell."

And then, as I pull my own incredulity back, I realize that apparently this thought never crossed Joseph's mind. Perhaps Joseph never justified having a bad attitude or a sad disposition, even though he was in prison.

When we read the Word of God, we must use it as a mirror to look at our own lives and into our own hearts. Are you aware of the troubles others face when dealing with your own wretched circumstances? Or are you so consumed with your deep disappointment that you forget others are battling discouragement as well? You can be pitiful, or you can be powerful, but you will never be both.

Your confinement is not about you. The hard place you are in may not soften until you begin to help someone else out of their human pain. You might be in the prison of affliction simply as a God-given opportunity to encourage someone else in a similar hard spot.

God Can Use Me in This Place

Several years ago, I was in a battle for my very life as cancer invaded my body. It seemed that every time I went to the doctor after a surgery or received test results, the news was worse than the visit before. The cancer was aggressive, and my doctors took serious measures. I couldn't believe cancer had the nerve to interrupt my plans and I wondered about the purpose of the battle.

As I prayed with my husband and searched out wisdom from Scripture, I realized that God could use me in this place. Ever since I was a little girl, I had asked the Lord to let me take His joy and hope to dark places. What place is darker and more despondent than a cancer hospital? What place is more discouraging than an oncology office?

I knew I had discovered my assignment in a situation I didn't like and would not have chosen. I decided to be a dispenser of encouragement and hope to every patient I encountered, every surgeon I met, every technologist assigned to me, and to every nurse who walked me down the hall. The battle was no longer about me—it was about them. I had been assigned to bring the gladness of the Lord to people who might not have heard the story of Jesus.

I am over seven years removed from my healing journey and today, my body is cancer-free. My doctors expected me to die but God intervened with His miracle-working power. I now look back at the span of over two years when I fought to survive, and I can affirm they were among the most joyful years of my entire life. I found joy in the dungeon of cancer.

⏳   *Can you look back at your life and remember a situation in which the Lord used you even though you were dealing with pain?*

⏳   *Are you brave enough to pray with a stranger? Ask the Lord to give you the opportunity to encourage someone and pray with them this week.*

Hidden Treasure: Read this verse out loud several times today and write it out on a 3x5 card. Think about this verse throughout the week and begin to commit it to memory:

As each one has received a special gift, employ it in serving one another as good stewards of the manifold grace of God.

—1 Peter 4:10

Let no one go to hell unwarned and unprayed for.

—attributed to Charles Spurgeon

Day 2

It Matters

The meanwhiles in life are inevitable. We will all experience a meanwhile, regardless of our gender, our commitment to Christ, our socioeconomic level, or our education. However, we can determine what we *do* during the meanwhiles. The action you take during your meanwhile matters—it matters very much. Just ask Joseph.

The baker and cupbearer each had a dream on the same night in the same prison cell. Although their dreams were different in nature, they were both disturbed by these nocturnal visions.

> *Then they said to him, "We have had a dream and there is no one to interpret it." Then Joseph said to them, "Do not interpretations belong to God? Tell it to me, please."* **(Genesis 40:8)**

The cupbearer and baker couldn't figure out the meaning of their individual dreams and when Joseph asked about them, Joseph knew God could interpret. Joseph knew nothing was too difficult for his God. When faced with a dilemma in life, Joseph called upon the expertise of the Lord with no hesitation at all. Joseph directed these two prisoners to look to God for their answers.

The truth is, dreams were in Joseph's sweet spot. God had spoken to Joseph through dreams years before when he was but a youth in his hometown. We can see how Joseph matured, because he is careful to honor the Lord with his words as he speaks with the two prisoners. Joseph refused to take credit for his gift but honored God with his verbiage.

I believe this is a secret to life—no matter what your talent, exercise extreme caution and do not to take credit for it. Any gift, talent, or ability of yours did not originate from your stellar gene pool—it came from the Father. So, give Him the glory He deserves as you serve others with your God-given abilities.

> *Every good thing given and every perfect gift is from above, coming down from the Father of lights, with whom there is no variation or shifting shadow.* **(James 1:17)**

⏳   *What are the three main gifts you believe God has given to you?*

1. _____

2. _____

3. _____

⏳   *If you don't know, ask a friend or a family member what they believe your gifts or talents are.*

You are Important to Me

Joseph spent his meanwhile encouraging others and using his God-given gifts to bring hope to people who were discouraged. He didn't waste his meanwhile; instead, he turned it into a ministry. The ability to encourage someone might start with a simple question, "How are you doing?" just as Joseph did with the cupbearer and baker.

⏳   *What question could you ask someone who is going through a hard time to open a conversation of encouragement?*

I have a friend who is a pastor's wife and I watch her life with grand interest, so rich is her faith and so bold is her witness. When Diane and I go to a restaurant together, after we place our order with the waitress or waiter, Diane always takes off her glasses, looks the server intently in the face, then speaks kindly. She says, "In just a minute, Carol and I are going to pause and pray and thank God for our food. When we pray, is there anything we can pray for you?"

A Vine

In his dream, the cupbearer had seen a vine with three branches upon it. All three of the branches were producing buds which grew into blossoms and then into fruit or grapes.

> *So the chief cupbearer told his dream to Joseph, and said to him, "In my dream, behold, there was a vine in front of me; and on the vine were three branches. And*

as it was budding, its blossoms came out, and its clusters produced ripe grapes. Now Pharaoh's cup was in my hand; so I took the grapes and squeezed them into Pharaoh's cup, and I put the cup into Pharaoh's hand." (Genesis 40:9–11)

Note the cupbearer's explanation that in his dream he was holding Pharaoh's cup. As he did, he took the grapes and squeezed them and then placed the cup into Pharaoh's hand. This will prove important in Joseph's deciphering.

Then Joseph said to him, "This is the interpretation of it: the three branches are three days; within three more days Pharaoh will lift up your head and restore you to your office; and you will put Pharaoh's cup into his hand according to your former custom when you were his cupbearer. Only keep me in mind when it goes well with you, and please do me a kindness by mentioning me to Pharaoh and get me out of this house." (Genesis 40:12–14)

Joseph was able to interpret the dream of the cupbearer through the wisdom of God. He told the man that the three branches symbolized three days. Within those three days, Pharaoh would intervene, releasing the cupbearer from imprisonment, restoring him to his former position in the king's court. Joseph made just one personal request of the cupbearer, that he would remember Joseph and put in a good word for him. Joseph was hoping the servant would be as kind to Joseph as Joseph had been to him. This request touches me deeply. I believe it was a valid, humble, and completely understandable request made by the falsely imprisoned Joseph.

Joseph's Side of the Story

For the very first time in the narrative of Joseph, we are about to hear his side of the story. Even as Joseph explains to the cupbearer why he is in prison, he is not vindictive; he simply and clearly states the facts.

For I was in fact kidnapped from the land of the Hebrews, and even here I have done nothing that they should have put me into the dungeon. (Genesis 40:15)

As you read these ancient words, doesn't your heart go out to Joseph? Don't you feel a dose of compassion for this young man and his tattered life? I tend to be a fixer and I want to mend Joseph's circumstances. However, God's ways are much higher than my ways and although I would have instantly released Joseph from prison, God had a better plan.

There is one more important teaching lesson in this passage that bears our consideration. Did you notice Joseph's humility, even in presenting his personal case to the cupbearer? He didn't talk about the ill-treatment of his brothers or the wrong done to him by Potiphar's wife. He simply said, *"I am innocent."*

Even when it is appropriate for us to vindicate ourselves, we should never malign the character of others.

⧗   *Have you ever tried to give God advice? Has He taken it?*

⧗   *Have you ever used these words when talking to God:*
      "Well, God, if You would just . . ."?

It is in the most devastating circumstances that we must fully and completely trust the timing of God and His ways. It's called surrender.

White Bread

Now let's discuss the baker. He was thoroughly impressed with Joseph's ability to interpret the dream of the cupbearer, so he wanted a turn at having his deciphered.

> **When the chief baker saw that he had interpreted favorably, he said to Joseph, "I also saw in my dream, and behold, there were three baskets of white bread on my head; and in the top basket there were some of all sorts of baked food for Pharaoh, and the birds were eating them out of the basket on my head." (Genesis 40:16–17)**

In the baker's dream, he was holding three baskets on his head. In the top basket were all sorts of pastries and delicacies for Pharaoh. The birds eating out of the basket provides an interesting detail. I wonder if Joseph paused thoughtfully and then prayed for strength before he was forced to give the unsuspecting baker this interpretation:

> **Then Joseph answered and said, "This is its interpretation: the three baskets are three days; within three more days Pharaoh will lift up your head from you and will hang you on a tree, and the birds will eat your flesh off you." (Genesis 40:18–19)**

Can you imagine having to say these words to a man whom you knew well—someone who had been under your charge? The interpretation of the baker's dream was devastating. Joseph likely looked the baker compassionately in his eyes and quietly told him the three baskets represented three days. Joseph had to inform this man, who I imagine had become more than a cellmate, that within three days Pharaoh would hang him and the birds would eat his flesh.

⧗   *How can you frame your words when you are required to bring bad news to a person whom you care about?*

⧗   *What are some of the character traits necessary to engage someone in a difficult conversation?*

Sure Enough

Within three days, it happened just as Joseph said it would. The cupbearer was restored to a position of prominence in the king's palace and the cup was back in his hand. The chief baker was hanged on a tree. God had spoken through Joseph.

> *Thus it came about on the third day, which was Pharaoh's birthday, that he made a feast for all his servants; and he lifted up the head of the chief cupbearer and the head of the chief baker among his servants. He restored the chief cupbearer to his office, and he put the cup into Pharaoh's hand; but he hanged the chief baker, just as Joseph had interpreted to them. (Genesis 40:20–22)*

When I read this story that is thousands of years old, I can't help but wonder a few things. Would you like to wonder with me?

⧗   *I wonder if the other prisoners had heard Joseph's conversations with the cupbearer and baker.*

⧗   *I wonder why we are told it was Pharaoh's birthday on this third day.*

⧗   *I wonder if Joseph's reputation in prison became even more admirable due to the way he handled this situation.*

⧗   *I wonder.*

Another Meanwhile

Do you think that perhaps Joseph breathed a huge sigh of relief when the dreams came to reality just as he had said? Do you suppose Joseph might have thought, *At last. The cupbearer will defend my character to Pharaoh and I will be released from jail. My meanwhile is just about over.*

> **Yet the chief cupbearer did not remember Joseph, but forgot him. (Genesis 40:23)**

This verse is nearly too painful to read, isn't it? We have fallen in love with the young man who was favored by his father, bullied by his brothers, sold into slavery, lost an unprovoked sexual harassment case, and is now forced to spend even more time in prison. As I read the account, I often find myself thinking, *God, where are You in Joseph's story? When will you show up?*

But I believe the Father quietly answers my frustrating questions by saying, *Carol, you can trust that I am in Joseph's story just as I am in yours. I will show up at just the right time—for you and for Joseph.*

The verse above sets into motion yet another meanwhile for Joseph. He has gone from the pit to the caravan to Potiphar's house to prison. Now it seems his destiny is in the forgetful hands of an amnesiac.

Let me assure you that although the cupbearer may have forgotten Joseph—God has not. You may feel forgotten and ignored by the people around you, but you are God's number one priority.

Can a woman forget her nursing child And have no compassion on the son of her womb? Even these may forget but I will not forget you. Behold, I have inscribed you on the palms of my hands.

—Isaiah 49:15–16

⧗ *Spend some time meditating on our treasure verse. Ask God to show you the gifts He has placed with you.*

God is never late—He is never late. But I have never known Him to be early, either.

—Marilyn Hickey

Day 3

730 Long Days

Two full years—730 long days—have passed since the cupbearer was released from prison. Joseph is still a victim of misplaced justice, he remains in prison, and he is tethered to the forgetfulness of a person whom he helped. However, God has not forgotten Joseph and He will once again use a dream to direct Joseph's life.

> *Now it happened at the end of two full years that Pharaoh had a dream, and behold, he was standing by the Nile. And lo, from the Nile there came up seven cows, sleek and fat; and they grazed in the marsh grass. Then behold, seven other cows came up after them from the Nile, ugly and gaunt, and they stood by the other cows on the bank of the Nile. The ugly and gaunt cows ate up the seven sleek and fat cows. Then Pharaoh awoke. He fell asleep and dreamed a second time; and behold, seven ears of grain came up on a single stalk, plump and good. Then behold, seven ears, thin and scorched by the east wind, sprouted up after them. The thin ears swallowed up the seven plump and full ears. Then Pharaoh awoke, and behold, it was a dream. Now in the morning his spirit was troubled, so he sent and called for all the magicians of Egypt, and all its wise men. And Pharaoh told them his dreams, but there was no one who could interpret them to Pharaoh. (Genesis 41:1–8)*

Pharaoh had two consecutive dreams that troubled him greatly, so he called for the magicians who served the royal court in Egypt. These conjurers belonged to a group known as experts in handling the rituals of magic and what was known in Egypt as "priestcraft." These men would likely participate in witchcraft today. Even so, they were recognized as the wisest men in all of Egypt, yet even they were unable to interpret Pharaoh's dream for him. It makes me wonder . . . do you believe it is possible that God made the minds of Pharaoh's philosophers blank? After all, God had the power to plant the dreams even though Pharaoh did not worship the Lord. The fact is, God could have given the astronomers or magicians interpretations, but He chose not to.

⧗   *Have you ever had a dream in which God spoke to you?*

⧗   *Why do you believe God speaks through dreams?*

⧗   *Do you believe God still speaks through dreams today?*

⧗   *Why do you believe God chose not to give secular magicians the interpretations of Pharaoh's dreams?*

The Timing of God

One of the mysteries of life is the timing in which our good Father operates. This mystery is magnified in the story of Joseph's meanwhile. However, as we stand from a rich historical distance and watch this narrative unfold, we are satisfied with God's choices concerning His ultimate timing.

If the cupbearer had remembered Joseph upon his release from prison, Joseph would have almost assuredly gone back to the land of the Hebrews. But God required Joseph's services for a greater need and for an exact moment. As we continue to dig for gold in the story of Joseph, you can confidently know God's timing is always flawless perfection.

A Stirring Reminder

Reading this portion of the story provides a stirring reminder that we should never look to the world's so-called experts for solutions to our problems or answers to our questions. As we follow Christ in the twenty-first century, we must realize that reading secular magazines or watching network TV will never lead us into all truth. The world has no lasting solutions for you, my friend. All the answers you ache for concerning life, marriage, parenting, healthy living, and emotional stability are found in the Bible.

Grace and peace be multiplied to you in the knowledge of God and of Jesus our Lord; seeing that His divine power has granted to us everything pertaining to life and godliness, through the true knowledge of Him who called us by His own glory and excellence. For by these He has granted to us His precious and magnificent promises, so that by them you may become partakers of the divine nature, having escaped the corruption that is in the world by lust.

—2 Peter 1:2–4

Peter reminds in the verses above that, "His divine power has granted to us everything pertaining to life and godliness."

When your spirit is troubled, like Pharaoh's was in Genesis 41:8, consult a man or a woman of God for wisdom. When you need guidance concerning adversity or misfortune, read the Word of God in which hides the wisdom of the ages. How wonderful to know that when we pray about the confusion often surrounding earthly situations, He will answer us. At times, I have seen a certified Christian counselor for guidance and emotional stability. Other times, I have talked with one of my mentors or with a pastor and his wife, all of whom helped me peel back the layers of my pain until I was whole once again.

⧖ *Where do you go for help when you are troubled?*

⧖ *At what point in a challenging situation do you make the decision to see a counselor or pastor?*

⧖ *How is the treasure verse touching your heart this week? Have you shared it with anyone yet?*

As Christians we need to understand there are consequences for trusting in anything other than God, who is able to meet all our needs—natural or spiritual.

—David Odunaiya
How to Make Faith Work in Your Life

Day 4

A Moment of Clarity

Have you ever forgotten an extremely important detail due to busyness, distractions, or just plain absent-mindedness? I have, and when I ultimately remembered the thing I should never have forgotten, I was embarrassed and forlorn.

The chief cupbearer, after two long years, finally had a moment of recall and immediately went to Pharaoh.

> **Then the chief cupbearer spoke to Pharaoh, saying, "I would make mention today of my own offenses." (Genesis 41:9)**

The cupbearer is about to confess to Pharaoh what had happened to him when he dreamed a troubling dream during his time in the Egyptian dungeon:

> **Pharaoh was furious with his servants, and he put me in confinement in the house of the captain of the bodyguard, both me and the chief baker. We had a dream on the same night, he and I; each of us dreamed according to the interpretation of his own dream. Now a Hebrew youth was with us there, a servant of the captain of the bodyguard, and we related them to him, and he interpreted our dreams for us. To each one he interpreted according to his own dream. And just as he interpreted for us, so it happened; he restored me in my office, but he hanged him. (Genesis 41:10–13)**

I can imagine that the heart of the earnest cupbearer was beating out of his chest. Would he be hanged for overlooking this very important interaction? Or was the possibility of a promotion at play since he could introduce someone to interpret Pharaoh's dream? The cupbearer knew Pharaoh was an impetuous man and he had the power to either murder the cupbearer or elevate him. Which would it be?

This sets the stage for the cupbearer to humbly approach Pharaoh and confess the details of his own dream, and thus his release from prison.

⧗   *Do you struggle with the timing of God in your life?*

⧗   *What is the difference between living in time yet honoring and praying to a God of eternity?*

A Humble Response

The palace staff hurried to release Joseph from prison but before they brought him to Pharaoh, they gave him new clothes as well as a bath and a good haircut. When Joseph was physically ready, he stepped into the throne room of Pharaoh, the man who was considered to be god incarnate by all under his rule.

> **Then Pharaoh sent and called for Joseph, and they hurriedly brought him out of the dungeon; and when he had shaved himself and changed his clothes, he came to Pharaoh. Pharaoh said to Joseph, "I have had a dream, but no one can interpret it; and I have heard it said about you, that when you hear a dream you can interpret it." Joseph then answered Pharaoh, saying, "It is not in me; God will give Pharaoh a favorable answer." (Genesis 41:14–16)**

As Joseph begins to understand why he was called to an audience with Pharaoh, he immediately makes his position clear. *"It is not in me; God will give Pharaoh a favorable answer."*

Joseph wasted no time with undue pride or showmanship. The first words out of his mouth in Pharaoh's presence gave honor to the God whom he served so passionately. My heart just aches with appropriate pride as I hear Joseph's gentle voice in the throne room of Pharaoh.

⧗   *When you are in a conversation with someone who does not know the Lord, what are your main goals?*

⧗   *What does it mean to you to "hear from God and give glory to God"?*

An Earnest and Peaceful Statement

Joseph told the anxious ruler that God would surely give him a "favorable" answer. The word Joseph used is *shalom* or *peace*. Joseph already knew, before even hearing the dream, that the Lord would use him as an instrument and messenger of peace. In all situations, Joseph's role is our role. Our words should bring calmness to anxiety and insight to uncertainty. Our life should provide a peaceful demonstration of the character of God. When one of God's children arrives on the scene, the atmosphere should automatically be charged with serenity and the answers only He can offer.

⧗   *What does it mean to be a messenger of peace?*

⧗   *Is it possible to deliver God's presence to every situation? Why or why not?*

If you read between the lines of Joseph's statement, *"It is not in me; God will give Pharaoh a favorable answer,"* you can hear his earnest heart making one thing clear from the very beginning. He was a man of God, who listened to God and who honored Him. If any pride existed at all in Joseph as a boy, it had now disappeared.

When a man or woman of God is required to spend time in a meanwhile of life, all pride is stripped away, isn't it? Anything that had been raw about Joseph was now refined and pure. Joseph was no longer strutting his stuff. He was a humble man keenly aware of his own humanity and yet the greatness of the God whom he served.

⧗   *What has a meanwhile in life done to you emotionally?*

⧗   *What has a meanwhile in life accomplished in you spiritually?*

Meanwhile seasons have matured me, strengthened me, humbled me, and changed me. Time spent in the meanwhile of life cultivates compassion for another's pain and wisdom for the rest of the journey. After a man or a woman endures a meanwhile, somehow all that really matters afterward is honoring God through the words one speaks, the emotions one demonstrates, and the actions one chooses.

Joseph stood in front of the great and powerful Pharaoh a changed man. He was no longer dressed in prison garb, and probably shaved in the Egyptian custom. Joseph might have appeared Egyptian on the outside, but make no mistake, my friends, Joseph was a Hebrew, son of the Most High God through and through.

⧗   *Remember to linger over our treasure verse for the week and allow God to speak to you concerning your gifts and talents. Today would be a good day to give everything you are and everything you have to God once again.*

Spread out your petition before God, and then say,
"Thy will, not mine, be done." The sweetest lesson
I have learned in God's school is to let the Lord
choose for me.

—D. L. Moody

Day 5

Pacing in the Palace

Pharaoh is in his throne room and this powerful man is visibly troubled in his spirit. He is likely pacing back and forth filled with anxiety and fear. He has just been the victim of two horrible nightmares—they've haunted him day and night. He has gone to the most esteemed minds in his entire kingdom, and no one can help him. No one is able to interpret his dreams.

The cupbearer had a moment of recall in which he remembered the young Hebrew prisoner who had interpreted his own troubling dream at least two years earlier. Joseph was called up from the dungeon, shaved, and given appropriate clothes to wear in the fearsome leader's presence.

> *So Pharaoh spoke to Joseph, "In my dream, behold, I was standing on the bank of the Nile; and behold, seven cows, fat and sleek came up out of the Nile, and they grazed in the marsh grass. Lo, seven other cows came up after them, poor and very ugly and gaunt, such as I had never seen for ugliness in all the land of Egypt; and the lean and ugly cows ate up the first seven fat cows. Yet when they had devoured them, it could not be detected that they had devoured them, for they were just as ugly as before. Then I awoke. I saw also in my dream, and behold, seven ears, full and good, came up on a single stalk; and lo, seven ears, withered, thin, and scorched by the east wind, sprouted up after them; and the thin ears swallowed the seven good ears. Then I told it to the magicians, but there was no one who could explain it to me." (Genesis 41:17–24)*

I wonder if Joseph listened intently to the words of Pharaoh and prayed silently for God to speak to him. Joseph was likely not impressed by the grandeur or opulence of the throne room even though he had spent the last several years in a dark, dank dungeon. I imagine Joseph stared steadfastly at the face of Pharaoh; his ears were attuned to every word and intonation that came out of the mighty man's mouth. Perhaps Joseph's heart was racing knowing this would be his only opportunity to escape the horrid living conditions in the jail. Or maybe, he was more aware of the importance of honoring God whether he was ever released from prison or not.

⧗   *How do you respond to tense situations?*

The Exclamation Point of God

God spoke through a Hebrew prisoner by the name of Joseph. A man whose heart was in tune with the heart of his Creator, able to clearly hear God's voice and then repeat the knowledge of God.

> **Now Joseph said to Pharaoh, "Pharaoh's dreams are one and the same; God has told to Pharaoh what He is about to do. The seven good cows are seven years; and the seven good ears are seven years; the dreams are one and the same. The seven lean and ugly cows that came up after them are seven years, and the seven thin ears scorched by the east wind will be seven years of famine. It is as I have spoken to Pharaoh: God has shown to Pharaoh what He is about to do. Behold, seven years of great abundance are coming in all the land of Egypt; and after them seven years of famine will come, and all the abundance will be forgotten in the land of Egypt, and the famine will ravage the land. So the abundance will be unknown in the land because of that subsequent famine; for it will be very severe. Now as for the repeating of the dream to Pharaoh twice, it means that the matter is determined by God, and God will quickly bring it about." (Genesis 41:25–32)**

Joseph didn't hesitate nor did he negotiate. He humbly and thoroughly repeated every word God had laid in his young heart. The former prisoner, Joseph, demonstrated a soul free and at rest. He was not constrained by his disappointment nor defined by his circumstances. He was an unencumbered man who kept his gaze singularly on his Lord. Whatever chains had held him in prison had no power over his spirit.

⧗   *Can you say you are free regardless of your circumstances?*

⧗   *What does it mean to live a life of freedom even when dealing with monumental pain?*

I like to call the interpretation of Pharaoh's dream *"the exclamation point of God!"* Our Father would have the last word in this story.

A Historical Side Note

Egypt was extraordinarily wealthy during the years of Joseph's slavery and imprisonment. The land was exceptionally fertile due to the yearly inundation of the Nile which delivered rich topsoil to the valley and delta regions. Practically anything grew in Egypt. Due to the plentiful Nile water and long days of sunshine, most fields produced two abundant crops each year.

The land was also rich in natural resources. Fish and waterfowl were plenteous in the river while game was found in the desert. Papyrus, clay, limestone, copper, and gold were all abundant in this ancient nation.[12]

Hence, for Joseph to prophesy a famine seemed absurd. It's doubtful this prosperous nation even knew what a famine was.

A Poignant Prophetic Word

As I ponder the preceding passage of scripture, verse 32 is especially poignant to me.

> **Now as for the repeating of the dream to Pharaoh twice, it means that the matter is determined by God, and God will quickly bring it about. (Genesis 41:32)**

Although Joseph's deliverance was not brought about quickly by God, we sense no guile or blame in the spirit of Joseph. Joseph was able to sincerely inform Pharaoh that God would work quickly in the matter he had dreamed. Although Joseph may not have wondered why he was still in prison based upon the authority and unction of God, *I certainly wonder why.*

Joseph was a man who chose to trust in the ways and in the timing of God. This is something God must work out in our human hearts. We must mature and know in our spirits that we can trust the timing of God. I have heard Bible teacher Marilyn Hickey say, "God is never late, but I have never known Him to be early either."

⌛ *Can you think of a Bible verse that will help you trust the Lord to a greater degree when it comes to matters of timing?*

I wonder if, even as Joseph spoke the heart of the Father to Pharaoh, he was thinking about the fact that his personal deliverance had not happened quickly. Years had passed since he had heard the voice of his father or had known physical freedom. Regardless, Joseph continued with the rest of Pharaoh's dream interpretation:

"Now let Pharaoh look for a man discerning and wise, and set him over the land of Egypt. Let Pharaoh take action to appoint overseers in charge of the land, and let him exact a fifth of the produce of the land of Egypt in the seven years of abundance. Then let them gather all the food of these good years that are coming, and store up the grain for food in the cities under Pharaoh's authority, and let them guard it. Let the food become as a reserve for the land for the seven years of famine which will occur in the land of Egypt, so that the land will not perish during the famine."

Now the proposal seemed good to Pharaoh and to all his servants. (Genesis 41:33–37)

Not only did Joseph interpret the dreams for Pharaoh, but he also tapped into the wisdom of all eternity in offering advice, because he had a submissive spirit and knew the Father intimately. Joseph was more aware of the Lord's presence than he was of his human pain. Joseph was also more aware of the Lord's presence than he was of the intimidating human ruler in the room.

My friend, I have learned I cannot tap fully into the knowledge of the Father as long as I insist on demanding my own way according to my own time preference. If Joseph had spent the past several years shouting, *"I hate this prison! This prison is so unfair! I don't deserve this prison! It stinks in here and the food is horrible!"* he never would have had the capacity to connect with the heart of God when it mattered the most.

⧗   *How can we tap into the wisdom of God? Be practical.*

So it is with all of us who currently live on the earthly side of heaven's glory. We will never know God's powerful answers when we are demanding our own way. When others mistreat us, if we justify our bad behavior such as gossip, revenge, or blame with cultural influence or with secular psychology, we will deny ourselves the blessing of being the beneficiary of the mind of God.

A man's gift makes room for him
And brings him before great men.

—Proverbs 18:16

Joseph used his God-given gifts whether he was living in the comfort of home, as an indentured slave, in the dungeon, or in the throne room. He didn't make excuses or shy away from using his talents to serve others.

⧗   *What is one gift you want to offer to the Lord today?*

⧗   *Write out a prayer of surrender as you contemplate how the Lord will use this gift for His kingdom purposes.*

Joseph encouraged Pharaoh to appoint a man who was discerning and perceptive over the agriculture of Egypt. This would require quite a feat because Pharaoh had been unable to find anyone competent to interpret his dream among the wisest and most respected men in the entire land. Who would help Pharaoh prepare for a seven-year famine?

I don't believe Joseph was promoting himself for the job—a slave running the land would have been preposterous. Joseph was merely repeating to Pharaoh what God had spoken to his soft and pliable heart.

The truth is, Joseph had experienced circumstantial famine ever since the day his brothers sold him into slavery. A glorious new day was about to dawn in the life of Joseph.

⧗   *Have you memorized the treasure verse from this week? Take a minute to write it out in your own words:*

So live for the kingdom of God. Seek to bring glory to Jesus Christ and the Lord will use you. It is my prayer, my constant and daily prayer, that God would keep me useable.

—Chuck Smith
Calvary Chapel Distinctives

THE JOSEPH PRINCIPLE

Barbara Johnson

Barbara Johnson was given an extraordinary life filled with the stuff of which most women only dream. Born in 1927, Barbara, as a young woman, married the man of her dreams, had four lively sons in succession, and by the early 1950s was living, literally, the great American dream. The Johnsons were active in their community and church as youth leaders.

In 1966, the entire Johnson family prepared to go with their church on the annual youth retreat in the mountains of California. Barbara's husband, Bill, was driving alone while Barbara had the two youngest sons in the car with her. Their two teenaged boys rode with the youth group in the church van. About ten miles from the resort site, Barbara's headlights beamed on the figure of a large man lying in the middle of the mountain road covered in his own blood. Although he was unidentifiable due to horrific head injuries, Barbara knew him, because she had ironed the shirt he was wearing only hours before. It was her beloved husband and best friend, Bill.

The prognosis was not good, but Bill lived through the unending night. Physicians gently told Barbara there was extensive brain damage and although he might live, the old Bill would be gone. After a week of vigilant prayers, the doctors informed Barbara that Bill was permanently and completely disabled. He might even be a blind vegetable for the rest of his life, never to leave the hospital. But Barbara knew she served a God who delights in touching broken people and making them whole again. So began Barbara's journey into deepening her faith.

Barbara and her family adopted the words of Jesus from Mark 10:27 as their fighting theme in this tragic situation:

> **With people it is impossible, but not with God; for all things are possible with God.**

One year later, after days of faith and failure, tears and laughter, therapy both mental and physical, and a relentless belief in a powerful God, Bill returned to work as a full-time mechanical engineer. He had been healed in spirit and body.

For one short year, the Johnson family settled back into a normal but much more thankful routine. Then in 1968, Barbara and Bill's oldest son, Steve, joined the U.S. Marines and was sent to Vietnam. Steve loved the Lord with his whole heart, and although the parting was painful, it was also peaceful. On July 28, 1968, the Johnson family learned that their eldest son was safe in the arms of Jesus.

In the summer of 1973, Tim, their second son, took off in a Volkswagen with two friends to "find himself." They spent the summer wandering through Alaska and not only did Tim find himself, but he also found Jesus Christ. Tim joined a church fellowship in Alaska, was baptized there, and gave his testimony one night in church. Tim was a changed young man filled with the Holy Spirit and with purpose and direction. The desire of Tim's heart was to come home at the end of the summer and rebuild some bridges he had unfortunately burned. The new Tim wanted to spend time with his parents and two younger brothers.

On the night of August 1, 1973, Tim's blue VW was crumpled in a head-on collision with a drunk driver on the wrong side of the road. Tim was instantly ushered into the arms of his Savior.

In June of 1975, Barbara and Bill discovered that David, their third son, had embraced a gay lifestyle. He then disappeared into the homosexual community for eleven years with no contact at all with his family. Can you imagine being Barbara Johnson?

How does a woman, a mother, go through such horrendous circumstances and not lose her mind? If your name is Barbara Johnson, you start a joy box.

Barbara's joy box was just a little shoebox she began filling with things that brought her joy. When a note from a friend arrived in the mail, she put it in her joy box. When she found a particularly comforting scripture verse, she wrote it on a card and put it in her joy box. She found a book of jokes from when the boys were little and stuffed that in her now overflowing box. Spring flowers from the yard went in along with a favorite recipe or two.

When her pieces of joy outgrew the shoebox, Barbara bought a plastic tub and began filling it with little pieces of life that stirred up joy. When her joy memorabilia no longer fit in her dozens of bins, she emptied their guest bedroom, and it became her joy room. When the guest bedroom could no longer hold it all, Bill built an addition onto their California ranch home to store all the notes, poems, music, pictures, scriptures, and other mementos that reminded Barbara and Bill they served a God of joy.

When a car accident nearly took Barbara Johnson's husband's life, she filled his hospital room with scriptures, quoted the Word of God over him, and had her sons memorize scriptures to pray over their beloved dad.

When her first son was killed in Vietnam, she had a cassette tape made with Steve's life story on it. Barbara reached out to other grieving mothers who had lost sons and sent them the recording. Steve's story ended with the comforting hymn, "Safe in the Arms of Jesus."

When her second son, Tim, was killed, Barbara spoke in church that very Sunday morning. The altar filled with Tim's friends who gave their lives to Jesus.

When her son, David, disappeared for eleven years into the gay community, Barbara began Spatula Ministries to peel parents off the ceiling when their children broke their hearts.

Barbara's books have sold millions of copies and she changed hundreds of thousands of people's lives because of her testimony and refusal to give into depression and hopelessness. Her commitment to embrace joy at the very worst moments of her life took supreme diligence. But Barbara did it because of God's power given to her, and because she knew Him intimately.

We all choose how to walk out our faith. My prayer is that you will choose to press ahead in the face of insurmountable and seemingly impossible odds. I pray you step over hell with your face set like flint toward God's kingdom of joy and peace.

With so many cesspools to fall into in life, we need a spring we can go to for splashes of joy—a spring full of living water that only Jesus provides. The foundation of all joy for Christians is that we can live as though Christ died yesterday, rose today, and is coming tomorrow.

—Barbara Johnson
Splashes of Joy in the Cesspools of Life

Week 6

Heaven's Perspective
Changes Everything!

Day 1

Powerful Persuasion

Joseph is in the throne room with the great and terrible Pharaoh. God gave Joseph the wisdom to interpret Pharaoh's dream, but He also provided further advice for Joseph to offer the Egyptian leader.

After providing the interpretation, Joseph humbly but directly presented godly counsel to Pharaoh about dealing with the imminent and fierce challenge ahead. The dreams of Pharaoh were interpreted to mean that Egypt would enjoy seven years of abundance followed by seven years of extreme food scarcity. The switch from feast to famine would take place quickly. But God had prepared Joseph.

God saw Joseph as a leader when his brothers were beating him up. God saw Joseph's potential when he was in the pit and riding along a dusty road in the Midianite caravan. God watched Joseph's life with grand anticipation when he was a servant in Potiphar's house and in the Egyptian prison. God's view of Joseph had not changed at all. God saw Joseph as a leader despite his circumstances, rather than because of them. Joseph was a man of honor and faith; therefore God was able to use him wherever he went and whomever he was with. God does not define you by your circumstances but by the faith in your heart.

For God sees not as man sees, for man looks at the outward appearance, but the Lord looks at the heart.

—*1 Samuel 16:7*

⌛ *What does it mean to you that "God does not interpret who you are by your circumstances but by the faith in your heart"?*

⌛ *Does 1 Samuel 16:7 bring you comfort or does it cause you to wonder what God sees in your heart?*

⧗   *What do you believe God sees in your heart?*

God views you through heaven's perspective. His gaze is upon you from the vantage point of eternity.

Where is THAT Man?

During the abundant years, I wonder how Joseph intended to convince successful farmers hauling in extraordinarily good crops to hand over 20 percent of their harvest to the government. Especially when famine was virtually unknown in this region of the world. This idea surely sounded ridiculous, and I wonder if the counselors and wise men of Pharaoh, who were likely in the throne room with him as he shared this godly wisdom, rolled their pompous eyes at the bravado of this kid straight from prison.

> *"Now let Pharaoh look for a man discerning and wise, and set him over the land of Egypt. Let Pharaoh take action to appoint overseers in charge of the land, and let him exact a fifth of the produce of the land of Egypt in the seven years of abundance. Then let them gather all the food of these good years that are coming, and store up the grain for food in the cities under Pharaoh's authority, and let them guard it. Let the food become as a reserve for the land for the seven years of famine which will occur in the land of Egypt, so that the land will not perish during the famine."*
>
> *Now the proposal seemed good to Pharaoh and to all his servants.* **(Genesis 41:33–37)**

What you and I know due to our historical perspective is that Joseph's idea was offered from an entirely different Throne Room altogether. The King of the Ages had spoken to Joseph, and this young man was simply downloading that insight to a very temporary ruler.

Would it even be possible to find a man with the stellar leadership qualities that Joseph's proposition required? Would he be able to convince the leading agricultural experts of the day to give one-fifth of their harvest and place it in government grain bins? Where was such a man?

The Throne Room

Before we discover who Pharaoh chooses, let's pause and examine the throne rooms where you spend the hours, days, and years of your life. Are you clearly aware of the ways and opinions of earthly culture while in denial over what heaven's opinion on an issue might be? If God were to speak to you with an extraordinary answer, as He did to Joseph, would you even be able to hear His voice?

⧗ *Are you in the habit of hearing God's voice?*

⧗ *How and where do you hear the voice of your good, good Father?*

If all you focus on is yourself, your requirements and disappointment, let me humbly present to you that you may be in danger of worshipping yourself rather than God. Do you spend the vast amount of your time in a throne room wallpapered with selfies? Do you plunge into action without consulting God? Do you analyze situations but forget to ask God for His analysis? Do you avoid decisions until you hear what other people think you should do while failing to ask God for His take on your choice?

What do you want, my friend? Do you want what you want . . . or do you want what God wants for your life?

I love this quote by one of my heroines of the faith, Elisabeth Elliot. "To pray, 'Thy will be done,' I must be willing, if the answer requires it, that my will be undone."[13]

Are you spending your life in the throne room of the kingdoms of this world? Or is your favorite throne room the throne room of self? The throne room of culture will tell you what is culturally and currently acceptable—the throne room of self focuses on personal feelings.

It is in the Throne Room of God that the Word of God has final and joyful authority.

My prayer for you is that you would spend all your days . . . all your moments . . . all your time in the Throne Room of God. This will require some important self-evaluation. You will need to ask yourself these probing questions:

⧗ *What voices do I primarily listen to?*

⧗ *How do I make a decision when life is hard?*

⧗ *What do I think about on a daily basis?*

⧗   *Do I justify decisions, thought patterns, or emotions?*

⧗   *Do I quickly apologize?*

⧗   *Do I quickly forgive?*

Joseph was more aware of the eternal Throne Room of God than he was of the throne room of Pharaoh, a transient ruler. Thus, Joseph wasn't intimidated by earthly influences; he lived solely to honor the heavenly One.

Hidden Treasure: Read this verse out loud several times today and write it out on a 3x5 card. Think about this verse throughout the week and begin to commit it to memory:

Now to Him who is able to do far more abundantly beyond all that we ask or think, according to the power that works within us, to Him be the glory in the church and in Christ Jesus to all generations forever and ever. Amen."

—Ephesians 3:20–21

We must be ready to allow ourselves to be interrupted by God.

—Dietrich Bonhoeffer
A Year with Dietrich Bonhoeffer

$$\mathcal{D}ay\ 2$$

One Good Man

Pharaoh surely pondered the advice offered to him by Joseph, fresh from the dungeon. Perhaps Pharaoh ceased pacing, ascended his throne, and quietly sat down. His mind may have scattered in a thousand places at once. The pervasive question was this, *Do I have a man on my team who will be able to do what this God of Joseph requires?*

Apparently, Pharaoh and his servants quickly discussed the plan because the Bible reports:

> **Now the proposal seemed good to Pharaoh and to all his servants. (Genesis 41:37)**

A Historical Side Note

At this time in history, Egypt was a pagan nation, thus the God of Joseph was a stranger to Pharaoh. The gods of Egypt were clustered around the three great natural forces of Egyptian life: the Nile, the land, and the cloudless sky with its perpetual sun. Egypt was noted for its skills in medicine so there were also numerous gods of healing.[14]

The following scripture clearly describes the religion of Egypt during Joseph's tenure there:

For since the creation of the world His invisible attributes, His eternal power and divine nature, have been clearly seen, being understood through what has been made, so that they are without excuse. For even though they knew God, they did not honor Him as God or give thanks, but they became futile in their speculations, and their foolish heart was darkened.
Professing to be wise, they became fools, and exchanged the glory of the incorruptible God for an image in the form of corruptible man and of birds and four-footed animals and crawling creatures.

—Romans 1:20–23

And into this confusing and pagan religious structure, Joseph arrives on the scene and starts talking about God. Next time you are in an intimidating situation where your Lord and Savior is not honored or known, remember the courage of Joseph and insert your faith into the conversation.

As I ponder how Joseph may have felt, perhaps in his early years as a slave in Egypt, he was told something similar to a saying we've all heard. *"When in Rome, do as the Romans do."* He could have capitulated and thereby adopted the Egyptian mentality, religion, and morality. However, Joseph's advancement in Egypt was due to his refusal to adopt their ways—he chose to cling to his Hebrew faith. Joseph held tight to his virtue and the presence of the Lord, even while in a foreign culture. The famed theologian F. B. Meyer wrote of Joseph, "Though stripped of his coat, he was not stripped of his character."[15]

Remember that you and I are symbolically Joseph in this historical account written in Scripture. We must cleave to our character and to the promise of God even when the culture we are living in is void of commitment to Christ.

The Breath of God

After Pharaoh thought a bit, he then called his servants together and asked them the question of the hour.

> *Then Pharaoh said to his servants, "Can we find a man like this, in whom is a divine spirit?"* (Genesis 41:38)

Pharaoh's first priority was not human wisdom or leadership skills, rather he was looking for a man with "a divine spirit." A more accurate translation of this verse is:

> *And Pharaoh said unto his servants, "Can we find such a one as this is, a man in whom the Spirit of God is?"* (Genesis 41:38 KJV)

The descriptive phrase "a man in whom the Spirit of God is" might be one of the most glorious illustrations in all of Scripture. In the Hebrew, it is *ruah Elohim* which means "on whom God has breathed." The Hebrew words *ruah* and *Elohim*, when used together, denote the breath of God and is often actually translated as "the Holy Spirit."

It was the *ruah* of God that hovered over the deep before Creation (Genesis 1:2). It was the *ruah* of God that breathed over the land at the end of the flood and caused the waters to dry up (Genesis 8:1). The Bible reports that Daniel possessed an excellent spirit (*ruah*) because he had made up his mind to serve the Lord in the midst of a heathen culture (Daniel 5:12, Daniel 6).

Have you allowed the breath of God to inspire your life? Have you asked the Holy Spirit to give you more strength than you could ever have on your own? Are you determined to live in such a way that all of creation will recognize the breath of God on your one glorious life?

It is not prideful to ask for God to breathe in you. It is a dynamic request and even a necessary one for all who deeply desire to be used of the Lord in the midst of their meanwhile.

⧗   *What does it mean for you to have the Holy Spirit breathe upon your life?*

⧗   *According to Scripture, what are some of the benefits of having the Holy Spirit as an indwelling presence in your life?*

Pharaoh soberly realized that human strength and knowledge would not sufficiently enable him to feed the population during the tenuous days ahead. He needed a man with the Spirit of the living God pouring through his very soul. Pharaoh was hoping he could partner with a man who had God's answers, God's mind, God's thoughts, and God's heart.

Do people see the same character in you that Pharaoh saw in Joseph? The only way anyone will ever see Joseph's nature in us is if our eyes and hearts are continually set on the Lord and not on our situation. We must view our meanwhiles through the lens of God knowing He is our miracle-working Father.

A Tense Room

Would you imagine with me for just a moment what the atmosphere might have felt like in the throne room of Pharaoh? Tension may have been pervasive in the emotional environment as the highest-ranking men on earth waited for an answer from the Egyptian ruler. Joseph probably took a step or two back, believing his job had been accomplished, as he yet waited for dismissal. He dared not leave prior to Pharaoh's permission for him to be excused. Pharaoh, dressed in grandeur, sitting on the highest throne in all the known world, was in a conundrum. What man on his staff could succeed at this gargantuan responsibility?

Pharaoh might have slapped the arm of his golden throne and jumped up with excitement. He may have pointed his bejeweled finger at Joseph, freshly shaved from prison, and exclaimed, *"It's you! It's only you! It must be you!"*

The Same Spirit

Joseph's life is about to change because of the *ruah Elohim* that was so very evident in him. Always remember, the same Spirit of God who hovered over the deep at creation and lingered over Joseph's promising life, also hovers over you.

> But if the Spirit of Him who raised Jesus from
> the dead dwells in you, He who raised Christ Jesus
> from the dead will also give life to your mortal bodies
> through His Spirit who dwells in you.
>
> —Romans 8:11

⧗ As you spend a few minutes meditating on the treasure verse for this week, what is the "power that works within you"?

⧗ How does it change your perspective of your meanwhile knowing that the "ruah Elohim" hovers over your life?

> When we pray for the Spirit's help . . . we will simply fall down at
> the Lord's feet in our weakness. There we will find the victory and
> power that comes from His love.
>
> —Andrew Murray
> The Prayer Life

Day 3

Second in Command

Pharaoh's sobered concern was suddenly turned to unbridled enthusiasm when he named Joseph as the second highest ranking official in all of Egypt.

> *So Pharaoh said to Joseph, "Since God has informed you of all this, there is no one so discerning and wise as you are. You shall be over my house, and according to your command all my people shall do homage; only in the throne I will be greater than you."* (Genesis 41:39–40)

The appointment of Joseph to the vice presidency of Egypt was unprecedented and shocking. I wonder if the other officials in the room gasped as Pharaoh made his surprising choice. *A young man? Fresh from prison? Not even an Egyptian?*

I want to explain to you what a completely mind-boggling choice this was from a twenty-first-century western perspective. Let's imagine that the president of the United States of America just had a preposterous dream and it kept him up at night. His chief of staff remembered a young man in prison who accurately interpreted a dream of his, so they summon this prisoner who is also a foreigner.

They clean up the incarcerated fellow, giving him a good haircut and a fine-looking suit to wear into the Oval Office. As this prisoner listens to the dreams of the president, he is quick to inform this world leader that he will try to hear from God on the matter.

The newly shaved prisoner listens, then tells Mr. President that the weather patterns are about to change worldwide. He informs the captivated commander in chief that America will first experience seven years of unprecedented abundance followed by a famine unlike anything the country has ever known. Mr. President knows he must have some expert help with this issue. As he ponders his options, he doesn't reach out to Harvard or Yale. He doesn't bring in Nobel Award winners or men and women with doctorates in agriculture from Cornell. Mr. President has observed something extraordinary in this foreign prisoner who is perhaps from Haiti, Afghanistan, or Mozambique, and he gives him the job. Think about it—the uproar would be enormous.

This is exactly what happened in the throne room of Pharaoh on the day he chose Joseph to be second in command in Egypt.

The *ruah Elohim* made a way where there seemed to be no way for Joseph. The Lord was with him in the pit, in prison, and now in the palace. Was Pharaoh's dream just the result of what he had eaten the day before? No, it was a dream sent by God Almighty for His purposes alone.

⧖   *What is the biggest surprise God has ever given to you?*

⧖   *What surprise would you like God to give you?*

Information from God

Pharaoh began his appointment of Joseph with these words, "Since God has informed you of all this . . ." Pharaoh realized that the God of Joseph held the answer to all the challenges Egypt was about to face. Perhaps what Pharaoh hoped to communicate to his advisors was the obvious fact that an ordinary person was not able to operate with this type of sacred wisdom. Joseph possessed in himself no intrinsic ability to solve huge problems, but God who was within him was more than able.

May I remind you that you serve the same God as Joseph did? What amazing information. The God who lived in Joseph also lives in you. As you tap into His power and knowledge, you, too, may be given assignments that make no sense in the natural. God is still looking for a few good men and a few good women who will honor Him in the midst of a secular culture and in spite of a meanwhile. Are you that woman?

⧖   *If you could do anything for the unshakable kingdom of God, what would you want it to be?*

Gobsmacked

Joseph, in one instant of time, went from being a sordid, disrespected prisoner with no hope of ever getting out of the dungeon, to the number two man in all of Egypt. Talk about a meanwhile miracle. This is it.

You shall be over my house, and according to your command all my people shall do homage; only in the throne I will be greater than you. **(Genesis 41:40)**

Joseph was considered the equivalent of vice president or perhaps prime minister. Things like this don't just happen every day, but they *do* happen when God intervenes in the affairs of mankind. The hand of God was moving in the life of Joseph, and we are in the grandstands of faith cheering him on.

I would humbly like to submit to you today, that Joseph knew he was number two—but not to Pharaoh. Joseph knew he was second in authority to God and to God alone. In the remaining narrative of Joseph's life in the book of Genesis, not one derogatory statement is made concerning him. He is only one of two other characters in Scripture that this can be said of—Daniel and Jesus. We, of course, know that neither Joseph nor Daniel were without sin as Christ was, but the resounding truth is that Joseph lived with immaculate honor.

⧖   *How do you acknowledge the authority of God in your life?*

⧖   *What are some of the choices you have had to make in order to honor the authority of God in your life?*

⧖   *As you meditate on the treasure verse today, make a list of what you are asking for the power of God to do.*

The sacred moments, the moments of miracle, are often the everyday
moments, the moments which, if we do not look with more than
our eyes or listen with more than our ears reveal only . . .
a gardener, a stranger coming down the road behind us, a meal
like any other meal. But if we look with our hearts,
if we listen with all our being and imagination . . .
what we may see is Jesus himself.

— Frederick Buechner
The Magnificent Defeat

Day 4

A Reminder

s we continue to dig for gold in the biblical account of Joseph, I want to remind you that his life represents who we all can become during the most unending and stressful times in life. Perhaps this is a good definition of the word meanwhile: *stressfully unending*. However, as we know by now, a trust relationship with the Lord takes the stress out of our meanwhiles and offers a sweet peace and unexplainable hope.

If you recall our initial treasure verse, you know the Old Testament was written for our encouragement and instruction.

For whatever was written in former days was written for our instruction, that through endurance and through the encouragement of the Scriptures we might have hope.

—*Romans 15:4 ESV*

As Joseph's life begins to turn around and as he walks in his God-ordained destiny, let's pray that the blessing and honor Father God gave to Joseph will be our stunning garment as well.

Pharaoh said to Joseph, "See, I have set you over all the land of Egypt." Then Pharaoh took off his signet ring from his hand and put it on Joseph's hand, and clothed him in garments of fine linen and put the gold necklace around his neck. (Genesis 41:41–42)

The king's signet ring was symbolic of his ruling power and authority. No one dared argue with the one who had in his possession the king's ring. As the ruling royal in Egypt, Pharaoh did not "sign" documents with a quill, but instead, he dipped his signet ring into wax and then placed the symbol of the king on the document. Pharaoh freely gave Joseph his power of attorney with the gift of the ring. Joseph could now sign the name of the king on decision-making legal papers. The king placed exorbitant trust in the man named Joseph.

⧗   *How does this detail in the narrative of Joseph add new dimensions to your understanding of what your King has given to you?*

You've Got the Power!

As a child of the Most High God, you too, have been given the power of your King.

Jesus summoned His twelve disciples and gave them authority over unclean spirits, to cast them out, and to heal every kind of disease and every kind of sickness.

—Matthew 10:1

⧗   *Do you believe as a modern-day disciple of Christ that you have this same authority? Why or why not?*

And He summoned the twelve and began to send them out in pairs, and gave them authority over the unclean spirits.

—Mark 6:7

⧗   *Let me ask you again now that you have read yet another verse, do you believe as a modern-day disciple of Christ you have been given this same authority? Why or why not?*

Let's continue to pause on the details of Joseph's life and fill our hearts and minds with what the New Testament reveals concerning our authority in Christ. This next passage of scripture is so glorious and rich that my eyes fill with tears every time I read it. Paul wrote the following words to the church at Ephesus from a Roman prison.

I pray that the eyes of your heart may be enlightened, so that you will know what is the hope of His calling, what are the riches of the glory of His inheritance in the saints, and what is the surpassing greatness of His power toward us who believe. These are in accordance with the working of the strength of His might which He brought about in Christ, when He raised Him from the dead and seated Him at His right hand in the heavenly places, far above all rule and authority and power and dominion, and every name that is named, not only in this age but also in the one to come. And He put all things in subjection under His feet, and gave Him as head over all things to the church, which is His body, the fullness of Him who fills all in all.

—*Ephesians 1:18–23*

I'd like to ask you to read the above passage from Ephesians not once, not twice, but three times in a row. Allow the words of this massive and eternal proclamation to wash over your soul. Paul, the wordsmith and academician, rolled out the red carpet of faith toward all of us who believe. He heard from the Holy Spirit on the matter and Paul earnestly prayed we would know who we are in Christ and comprehend the power we have been given. You are in submission to Christ and as a bonus, you have the power and authority of Christ. As modern-day disciples, we don't get to decide *what* to do but we do get to determine *Who* we serve. As we lay our lives down at His nail-scarred feet, His authority floods our humanity. We are then known as His ambassadors, living a life of unmatched power through heaven's authority.

⧖ *What does it require for you as a disciple of Christ to live in a place of tandem power with Him?*

What a Gift

We must not abandon Paul just yet. Let's linger just a little longer on his message given to the New Testament church before we rejoin Joseph in Pharaoh's throne room. The discussion Paul and the Holy Spirit had with the early church was not a one-time provision. So intent was Paul about convincing persecuted Christians that the authority and power of the Holy Spirit was at their daily disposal, he penned this to the church at Colossae.

For this reason also, since the day we heard of it, we have not ceased to pray for you and to ask that you may be filled with the knowledge of His will in all spiritual wisdom and understanding, so that you will walk in a manner worthy of the Lord, to please Him in all respects, bearing fruit in every good work and increasing in the knowledge of God; strengthened with all power, according to His glorious might, for the attaining of all steadfastness and patience; joyously giving thanks to the Father, who has qualified us to share in the inheritance of the saints in Light.

—Colossians 1:9–12

Just as Joseph received the king's signet ring as a symbol of his authority, you have been given the power and indwelling presence of the Holy Spirit enabling you to bring the authority of Christ to planet earth. What a gift.

⧗   *Make a list of the things Paul prayed for the early church in the above verses.*

1. _____

2. _____

3. _____

5. _____

6. _____

7. _____

8. _____

Another Tunic

Joseph no longer wore prison garments because he was a free man. You should wear the garment of praise because you have been set free from sin and shame—no more inhabiting the prison of loneliness, anxiety, or hopelessness. You can walk through life proudly wearing Christ's cloak of salvation.

The king gave Joseph yet another garment to replace the initial one provided when he was removed from prison. Pharaoh now required that Joseph be dressed in the royal manner of fine linen. Joseph's outer covering, once again, represents the garment of praise given to us by our chain-breaking Father. Joseph was stripped of the varicolored tunic his earthly father bestowed upon him, he had lost his servant's garment to Potiphar's wife, but now, Pharaoh presents him with attire reserved for royalty.

My friend, you are royalty. Your Dad is the King of Kings. Put on your garment of praise and sing loudly enough for the world to hear. Give voice to your one inimitable song. Refuse to go through life wearing the sackcloth of yesterday's disappointments. Your days of whining, grumbling, and complaining are now over—you are covered in praise. And may I just say, you look smashing in it.

A Family Heirloom

Pharaoh then placed a heavy, gold necklace on Joseph, representative of his affiliation with the royal family. This piece of stunning, heirloom jewelry surely marked the royal ancestry for generations. As a believer in Christ, when you were set free from the bondage of sin, invited into the Throne Room of God's presence, something stunning occurred. You were welcomed as an intimate member of the wonderful family of God.

In closing today, would you take a deep breath and enjoy the following scripture in its entirety? I have referenced it from time to time, but right now, as you contemplate all that is happening in the life of Joseph and all he represents to us who are now in Christ Jesus, I believe this passage will come alive in your spirit.

For this reason I bow my knees before the Father, from whom every family in heaven and on earth derives its name, that He would grant you, according to the riches of His glory, to be strengthened with power through His Spirit in the inner man, so that Christ may dwell in your hearts through faith; and that you, being rooted and grounded in love, may be able to comprehend with all the saints what is the breadth and length and height and depth, and to know the love of Christ which surpasses knowledge, that you may be filled up to all the fullness of God.
Now to Him who is able to do far more abundantly beyond all that we ask or think, according to the power that works within us, to Him be the glory in the church and in Christ Jesus to all generations forever and ever. Amen.

—Ephesians 3:14–21

⧗ *Take a minute or two to enjoy the treasure verse for this week.*

*When human reason has exhausted every possibility, the children
can go to their Father and receive all they need. . . . For only when you
have become utterly dependent upon prayer and faith, only when all human
possibilities have been exhausted, can you begin to reckon that God
will intervene and work His miracles.*

—Basilea Schlink

Day 5

The Joseph Blessing

Joseph's life was revolutionized in one stunning moment when God intervened. His meanwhile was now coming to a climactic conclusion as Pharaoh continued to shower this young man with blessings and favor.

> He had him ride in his second chariot; and they proclaimed before him, "Bow the knee!" And he set him over all the land of Egypt. Moreover, Pharaoh said to Joseph, "Though I am Pharaoh, yet without your permission no one shall raise his hand or foot in all the land of Egypt." Then Pharaoh named Joseph Zaphenath-paneah; and he gave him Asenath, the daughter of Potiphera priest of On, as his wife. And Joseph went forth over the land of Egypt.
>
> Now Joseph was thirty years old when he stood before Pharaoh, king of Egypt. And Joseph went out from the presence of Pharaoh and went through all the land of Egypt. (Genesis 41:43–46)

Joseph was given the honor of riding in Pharaoh's second chariot—he had *Air Force II* at his very disposal. Joseph not only dressed differently, ate differently, and lived differently than he had while in prison, but now he traveled differently as well. You and I have been given the miraculous vehicle of prayer in which to travel through life. We are not constrained by our circumstances or events. Prayer is our *Air Force II*. Prayer will take us to powerful places in stunning and unmatched style.

⧖ *What is the greatest answer to prayer you have ever experienced?*

⧖ *What are you currently praying for?*

A New Name

Was Joseph jumping up and down yet? Was he weeping for joy? Was he kneeling in awe of all that was happening? I've tried to imagine what the response of Joseph might have been based upon my own response. But we can be sure of this—Joseph's heart was thumping out of his handsome chest.

Pharaoh had not only given Joseph freedom, authority, new clothes, a family heirloom, and a vehicle in which to travel, but he also gave him a new name. One of the possible meanings of Joseph's new name was "God speaks giving life to the world."[16] Isn't that just extraordinary? Pharaoh declared Joseph's destiny over him with this brand-new name. God had spoken through Joseph and given him a plan to save the world during a famine. Joseph's name has also been translated to mean "Abundance of Life" and "God's Word Speaking Life."[17]

Did you realize that God wants to speak through you as well? *God deeply desires for His eternal life to live through your miraculous life, bringing joy to the world.* Would you read that sentence one more time? You have just read what God's will for your life is. I have summed it up in one glorious sentence.

⧗ *Write out the glorious italicized sentence above so you never forget it.*

Just as Joseph was given a new name by Pharaoh, you too, have been given a new name. When you offered yourself to the unshakable kingdom of Christ, your new name became *Beloved* and *Saved*. Your new name is *Free*, *Powerful*, and *Forgiven*.

⧗ *Can you think of another new name that you were given at salvation?*

The Blessing of the Throne Room

There is a wondrous blessing that comes to a man or woman who spends time in the Throne Room of the King of all Kings. First of all, everything about daily life changes in an instant. Those who choose to spend time in His presence are now set free from the pain of the past. They wear the garment of praise. They are transported by the vehicle of prayer.

The family lineage has been realigned. They are given authority and they have the honor of a new identity. Who wouldn't want that?

I wonder if Joseph was incredulously thinking, *Just hours ago I was in prison and now I am in charge of all Egypt!*

How does this dynamic change of events happen in the life of a man or woman who spends time in the Throne Room? It happens because we serve a God who always keeps His promises.

> *The Lord will accomplish what concerns me;*
> *Your lovingkindness, O Lord, is everlasting;*
> *Do not forsake the works of Your hands.*
>
> —*Psalm 138:8*

When God speaks, He will move heaven and earth on your behalf. He is able to change the hearts of rulers, jailers, husbands, and bosses. When you, as a daughter of God, walk through life with honor and integrity, you will receive the "Joseph Blessing." When you live with moral excellence and undeniable trust, the "Joseph Blessing" will follow you all of your days.

⧗ *What is the "Joseph Blessing"?*

⧗ *How do you receive the "Joseph Blessing"?*

You Just Can't Count It

In one ordinary man, at one terrible moment in human history, we observe the favor of the eternal God. Joseph was intent on tapping into the wisdom God had given to him in every hard place in life. Joseph refused to ignore the presence of God in the throne room or in prison. Due to the faithful resolve of Joseph, the blessings of God followed him wherever he went.

> *During the seven years of plenty the land brought forth abundantly. So he gathered all the food of these seven years which occurred in the land of Egypt and placed the food in the cities; he placed in every city the food from its own surrounding fields. Thus Joseph stored up grain in great abundance like the sand of the sea, until he stopped measuring it, for it was beyond measure.* **(Genesis 41:47–49)**

The prosperity was so enormous at Joseph's moment in Egyptian history, that they were unable to measure the wealth and the abundance. How does this happen? When an ordinary man or a common woman determines that he or she will partner with the eternal God to make a resounding difference at his or her moment in history, the extraordinary occurs.

⧖　*What difference would you like to make?*

⧖　*Write out a prayer that asks God to help you make that specific difference.*

⧖　*What is one practical step you can take today to begin making your difference?*

⧖　*It's treasure verse time. Read it and enjoy it. Pray it over your life today.*

The will of God is always joy.

—*Elisabeth Elliot*

THE JOSEPH PRINCIPLE

Darlene Deibler Rose

When Darlene Mae McIntosh was a mere ten years old, a missionary came to her church in Ames, Iowa. After delivering a stirring sermon, he gave an altar call to the teens and college-age students, begging them to give their lives to foreign missions. Darlene sat on the back row during the call and felt a firm but loving hand on her shoulder. However, when she looked around no one was there. Darlene focused her heart and attention once again on the fervent missionary who was imploring young people to give their lives to serving others on foreign soil, but this time, she was unable to ignore the voice she heard audibly behind her. *Would you go anywhere for me no matter what the cost?*

Darlene, although only one decade old, walked bravely to the front and offered her life for the kingdom of God. She was the only one who responded that winter night.

After marrying Russell Deibler, a veteran missionary, in 1937, Darlene and Russell landed in Batavia, Java, on August 18, 1938, their first wedding anniversary. Married barely more than four years when Pearl Harbor was attacked, within two months, Darlene and Russell were abducted by the Japanese as prisoners of war.

The Deiblers were taken into the mountains by their captors on March 13, 1942. All of the men in their group were viciously beaten. The Japanese then came to take the bruised and battered men to a different location. As Darlene's young, injured husband was loaded into the back of the enemy's truck, he said to her, "Remember one thing, dear. God said He would never leave us or forsake us." Darlene never saw her husband on earth again.

Darlene recalls that as the vehicle pulled away from the weakened group of women and children, she experienced complete peace. She believed Romans 8:28 means exactly what it says.

> **And we know that God causes all things to work together for good to those who love God, to those who are called according to His purpose.**

Darlene knew, in the deepest caverns of her heart, that her mighty God would work even this tragedy together for His highest good.

During her next three years of imprisonment, Darlene and her fellow captive missionaries were forced to eat dogs and rats to stay alive. They were held in shacks on the side of a remote mountain and knew without a miracle they would never be rescued.

One night during this awful time, Darlene heard a noise and went out into the hallway of the ramshackle building. There she saw a man in a black sarong holding a machete in his hand. She recognized him immediately as a pirate and savage murderer. Darlene was a petite woman in her early twenties, but she was also well acquainted with the power and strength that comes not from human resources, but from the Holy Spirit. She chased this daunting enemy out of her building and down the roadway.

On the mountain trail that night, an entire gang of men who had been marauding the captives' shacks and raping women wrought new terror. But when these enemies of the people of God saw Darlene, they ran in fear for their lives. As Darlene walked wearily, yet gratefully back to her primitive hovel, she quoted the following Scripture.

The angel of the Lord encamps around those who fear Him,
And rescues them.

—Psalm 34:7

Night after night the pirates came back to the village, but they only stood outside the shack in which Darlene lived. Not one dared enter it again.

Years later, when Darlene returned to New Guinea as a missionary after World War II, she met a young man who had been part of the vicious gang during the war. This handsome young man was now a Christian and served the Jesus of the Gospels. When Darlene asked him why the pirates had never again attacked her shack, but only stood outside and looked at it, he replied, "Because of all of those people in white who stood guard around your house night after night after night."

Toward the end of World War II, Darlene and her missionary friends held in captivity began to hear bombs drop at night. Each morning, they gathered up lifeless bodies and buried them on the side of the mountain.

One night, during an especially intense attack, Darlene threw herself down into the safety of a deep ditch. All of the captives elected a favorite spot they ran to during the shower of bombs, and Darlene's was this familiar cavity in the earth. However, on this particular night, God spoke to Darlene shortly after she nestled into her ditch. He told her to go back in the house and retrieve a Bible that belonged to one of the other women.

Darlene's own Bible had long been confiscated, but as a little girl she had memorized literally hundreds of verses of scripture. When her cruel captors confiscated her beloved Bible, it did not matter, because Darlene knew the joy of hiding God's Word in her heart.

As Darlene raced through the ebony night, explosive flashes came closer and closer to the encampment. She had clearly heard God's voice tell her to rescue the Bible and so she was determined to obey rather than stay in the safety of her ditch. After Darlene found the Bible and hurried back outside, the bombs began to subside, and the raid came to an end. Darlene helped others back into the barracks.

The next morning, she saw a woman sleeping on the floor rather than on her bed. This woman told Darlene she had tried to save her mattress during the previous night's attack, so she threw it over the spot where Darlene always hid in the ditch. When the woman had gone back to get it, she found her mattress destroyed by a bomb. The voice of God and the Word of God had literally saved Darlene's life.

Darlene was only twenty-six years old when the war ended. Allied soldiers came and rescued the missionary captives and Darlene left on the very last boat. As Darlene's ship pulled away from the war-torn shore, she thought to herself, *I will never come back here again. I am going home to America, and I will stay there with my family.* But while the land grew smaller, the natives whom she and her husband had led to the Lord gathered along the shoreline and began to sing loudly, "God be with you till we meet again."

In that instant, Darlene knew she would return to this land of her captivity, and yet the land of her truest destiny. Darlene began to yell from the deck of the boat, tears streaming down her cheeks, "I will come back! I will come as soon as I can!"

After living only a few short years in America, Darlene married another missionary, Gerald Rose. They spent forty more years in the jungles, because she had heard God's voice. Darlene obeyed in faith what God had spoken to her heart as a ten-year-old girl in Iowa. Darlene Rose lived a life of great abundance and joy because the supernatural was more real to her than what she saw with human eyes.

I want my sons to know, if ever difficult circumstances come into their lives, that their mother's God is still alive and very well, and His arm has never lost its ancient power.

— *Darlene Deibler Rose*
Evidence Not Seen

Week 7

The Past Meets the Future

Day 1

Forget and Remember

Ihave often wondered what residual, long-lasting pain may have haunted Joseph's heart. Certainly, he remembered the feeling and smell of his childhood home. He must have thought about times around the dinner table with his dad and eleven brothers. But did he recall the bullying? Did he also reflect on the day his brothers sold him into slavery? How much of his dreams lingered in his mind?

⧗   *What is one happy memory you have from your childhood?*

⧗   *What is one memory that haunts you?*

⧗   *What can you do to deal with this painful recollection?*

Two Bouncing Baby Boys

Joseph and his Egyptian wife had two bouncing baby boys before the famine hit the heart of Egypt. Joseph was no longer alone but had been given a family. The Lord restored what was stolen from him.

> ***Now before the year of famine came, two sons were born to Joseph, whom Asenath, the daughter of Potiphera priest of On, bore to him. Joseph named the firstborn***

Manasseh, "For," he said, "God has made me forget all my trouble and all my father's household." He named the second Ephraim, "For," he said, "God has made me fruitful in the land of my affliction." (Genesis 41:50–52)

Joseph lived in Egypt, married an Egyptian woman, and was second in command in the Egyptian royal hierarchy. However, Joseph gave his sons each a Hebrew name. By this one act, we know Joseph remembered his heritage.

Joseph named his first son Manasseh, which in Hebrew means, "God has made me forget all of my trouble and all my father's household." Although Joseph remembered the facts of his painful past, he allowed God to heal his memories from those days. Memories present a great challenge for women, don't they?

Often in life, we allow the past to haunt us for decades and hold us back from future fruitful living. When especially painful trauma or abuse happens, it can become crippling or even paralyzing.

I pray you learn this from the story of Joseph—regardless of how the first part of your life unfolded, you can joyfully look ahead to God's abundance and faithfulness. Refuse to stay stuck in your painful past and believe the Father for a triumphant future.

I know so many Christian women who wrestle fiercely with former rejection and mistreatment. Issues such as growing up in an alcoholic home, sexual abuse, bullying and emotional damage at the hands of others bind them. My friend, I know you may have experienced some or all of these things—and if so, they were real. They happened and they happened to you. Allow me to encourage you today. Go for counseling, employ a group of prayer warriors, read Christian books on the topic, or perhaps talk to your pastor and his wife. Do whatever it takes to leave your past in the past. Your pain should be part of your history but not a glaring part of your future. Ask God to help you forget the wounds of yesterday and to live a life filled with His abundance today.

I once did an in-depth study on the words "forget" and "remember" in the Bible. In that infamous nutshell, I learned I am supposed to forget my stuff and remember God's stuff. I can do that, can you?

Too often, we forget what should be remembered and we remember what should be forgotten. When dealing with painful memories, perhaps guiding questions could be:

⧖   *Is this event covered by the blood of Jesus?*

⧖   *Have I been forgiven for this?*

⧖   *Have I forgiven the person who caused my pain?*

⧖   *How can I remember the hand of God during this time in my life?*

⧖   *What good has come from this event?*

The practice of prayer and thanksgiving should be a vital aspect of daily spiritual disciplines. We must remember what God has done for us and praise Him for it every day. Scripture recounts many times when the people of God forgot who He was and what He had accomplished in their lives. When spiritual amnesia occurs, we are sure to lose our peace and perhaps our direction.

> *You neglected the Rock who begot you, And forgot the God who gave you birth.*
>
> *—Deuteronomy 32:18*

The prophet Isaiah lamented:

> *For you have forgotten the God of your salvation And have not remembered the rock of your refuge.*
>
> *—Isaiah 17:10*

Whatever else you might choose to remember, think about the blessings of God on your life and His perpetual presence with you. Don't ever forget to remember.

⧗ *List three blessings you are thankful for today.*

1. _____

2. _____

3. _____

⧗ *Tell someone about one of these blessings.*

Joseph named his second son Ephraim, or *"God has made me fruitful in the land of my affliction."* Joseph was gloriously declaring, through the birth of this second son, that the place of his former captivity was now the exact place of his greatest usefulness. Can you make that same declaration?

⧗ *If you had the opportunity to name children based upon what God has done in your life, what would you name them?*

Just So I Could Say It Every Day

My testimony is filled with pain, purpose, and God's overwhelming power. After giving birth to two little boys, oh, how Craig and I longed to expand our family again. I became pregnant when Matthew, whose name means "gift of God," was three and Christopher, "one who carries Christ," had just turned one. I couldn't wait to hold another baby in my arms. However, I lost this dear child at twelve and one-half weeks gestation.

Although my heart was broken, I knew I could become pregnant again, and so I did. This baby was delivered stillborn at fifteen weeks, and once more, grief entered my ravaged heart. My doctor felt I could carry a baby to term, so we conceived another child; however, for the third time, my pregnancy ended in death, not life. This little one was born at sixteen weeks. Despair overwhelmed me, and depression became an unwelcome guest in my heart.

After losing three longed-for babies, I became a patient at the Duke Infertility Clinic. The world-renowned specialist who treated me also encouraged my barren heart. He strongly believed his medical knowledge would help me carry a baby to term.

Even with the genius of medical science, our next baby died at twenty weeks in my womb and a fifth died at sixteen weeks. After losing five babies, four of whom I held in my hand, I was no longer able to get pregnant. My body just stopped ovulating. The depression was pervasive and strong.

My brilliant and caring doctor administered high doses of drugs to help me become pregnant and then monthly mega-doses of hormones to help me stay pregnant. Finally, after nearly seven long years of infertility, I gave birth to our third son, Jordan McLeod. Jordan means "the one who carries on" and Craig and I believed he would be the one to carry on our legacy of full-time ministry.

Yet still, I longed for another baby. I had always dreamed about and prayed for a large family. The months turned to years and even after extended high doses of fertility drugs, I was not pregnant. Not only did I feel my body had betrayed me, but I was also battling severe depression. My very wise doctor carefully said to me, "Carol, it's time. We have done enough. Your body needs a rest. Go home and enjoy the sons God has given to you."

And that's what I did. I decided to love being a "boy-mom" and gave my heart enthusiastically to the testosterone-filled home I had been granted.

God, however, as He often does, had different plans for my life. Two years later, I became pregnant with no medical intervention. What a miracle. We named her Joy, just so I could say the word *joy* every day.

And then, miracle of all miracles, three years later, when I thought I was going through menopause, I became pregnant with our fifth child. We named her, Joni Rebecca, after both of her grandmothers.

⧗   *If you could rename yourself, what would the name be?*

Hidden Treasure: Read this verse out loud several times today and write it out on a 3x5 card. Think about this verse throughout the week and begin to commit it to memory:

Now may the God of hope fill you with all joy and peace in believing, so that you will abound in hope by the power of the Holy Spirit.

—Romans 15:13

A baby is God's opinion that the world should go on.

—Carl Sandburg
Remembrance Rock

Day 2

Every Chapter, Every Verse, Every Word

The hope that we now observe and embrace in the life story of Joseph is at once pervasive and exciting. I can hardly wait to read what happens next to this boy who has grown up before our very eyes.

We've determined the Bible is true theologically and historically. When the Word of God says Moses parted the Red Sea, you can be sure it actually happened. When the Bible reports that the mouths of lions were closed the night Daniel spent in their den, you can know that you know those beasts didn't even lick their chops. When the Bible says Jesus turned the water into wine, you can cheer with all the guests at the wedding feast because the Word of God is true. Every chapter. Every verse. Every word.

⧗ *This is an important issue to settle in your soul. Do you believe the Bible is the inspired Word of God?*

God's History Book

An ancient tablet in Yemen verifies a seven-year time period of unmatched abundance in ancient Egypt. It was directly followed by a seven-year famine.

> *When the seven years of plenty which had been in the land of Egypt came to an end, and the seven years of famine began to come, just as Joseph had said, then there was famine in all the lands, but in all the land of Egypt there was bread. So when all the land of Egypt was famished, the people cried out to Pharaoh for bread; and Pharaoh said to all the Egyptians, "Go to Joseph; whatever he says to you, you shall do." When the famine was spread over all the face of the earth, then Joseph opened all the storehouses, and sold to the Egyptians; and the famine was severe in the land of Egypt. The people of all the earth came to Egypt to buy grain from Joseph, because the famine was severe in all the earth. (Genesis 41:53–57)*

Joseph heard and obeyed God's voice. The God of Abraham, Isaac, and Jacob was the God of our favorite son, Joseph. The world was in trouble at this moment in history, but a man of God had the mental and spiritual resources to provide for a world in need.

The world is in trouble, my friend, and it needs someone just like you and me to come to its assistance. We have the resources others are desperately lacking. We have the joy for which they are aching. We have the hope for which they are starving. We have the peace for which they are yearning. We have the abundance the world is craving.

In days of sorrow and of challenge, your home should be filled with people who urgently seek answers. In times of tragedy and political unrest, your life should be a safe haven for those who frantically beg for food to fill their souls.

Joseph made preparations, so when the famine arrived in Egypt, he was ready to feed the masses. Have you made the vital preparations in your life so you will be able to serve as an abundant resource for others who are living in emotional and spiritual famine? Stock up on the nutrients of God's Word for the express purpose of sharing it with others when they are living in the desert of circumstantial barrenness.

⏳ *What can you do to store up wisdom in preparation for giving it away?*

⏳ *What can you do to store up hope in case you need to share some of yours?*

⏳ *Do you have enough joy to appropriate for a world in deep sadness?*

Please don't miss the symbolism in the verses we just read. We live in a world suffering from the most debilitating famine known to mankind. People are starving to death and dying from a lack of eternal purpose, joy, hope, and peace. We are the ones with answers. As Christians in the twenty-first century, we must make ourselves available and share the spiritual wealth Christ has given to us. The days of hoarding and storing up have come to an end and the days of generous sharing must begin.

⧗   *What can you share with a world in pain?*

⧗   *In a practical sense, how will you do it?*

⧗   *Linger on the treasure verse for the week. Don't you just love this one? Make it part of your life today.*

We modern people think of miracles as the suspension of the natural order,
but Jesus meant them to be the restoration of the natural order.
The Bible tells us that God did not originally make the world to have disease, hunger,
and death in it. Jesus has come to redeem where it is wrong and heal the world where
it is broken. His miracles are not just proofs that he has power but also wonderful fore-
tastes of what he is going to do with that power.
Jesus' miracles are not just a challenge to our minds, but a promise
to our hearts, that the world we all want is coming.

— Tim Keller
The Reason for God

Day 3

Meanwhile . . . Back in Canaan

T he family of Joseph was suffering due to the worldwide famine. Jacob, the family patriarch, knew he must take serious action to provide for his family. Let's eavesdrop on a conversation taking place in Canaan at the homeplace.

> **Now Jacob saw that there was grain in Egypt, and Jacob said to his sons, "Why are you staring at one another?" (Genesis 42:1)**

Let's not miss the humor in this verse giggling from between Holy Spirit-inspired lines. Jacob, an old man now, looked at his assorted sons and knew there was not a leader among them. Not one of these middle-aged, balding men possessed the initiative or creativity needed to feed their families. None of these oblivious, selfish, overgrown boys has heard from God. The word *initiative* was foreign to the brothers and if Jacob left his sons in charge, the family would certainly starve to death. They simply sat around and stared at one another while their families waited, wretchedly hungry.

The verb used in this verse for "staring" is the Hebrew word *titrau* and it literally means "to face one another in combat." These hungry hulks were having a stare down right in front of their aged father. Apparently, the famine affected their morale, causing conflict among the brothers. Why doesn't THAT surprise us?

A Trust Issue

The last time Jacob had sent this pack of men out together, Joseph was killed. Jacob refused to take the same chance with Benjamin's life.

> **He said, "Behold, I have heard that there is grain in Egypt; go down there and buy some for us from that place, so that we may live and not die." Then ten brothers of Joseph went down to buy grain from Egypt. But Jacob did not send Joseph's brother Benjamin with his brothers, for he said, "I am afraid that harm may befall him." (Genesis 42:2–4)**

We can discern from this description of the family history that Jacob did not trust his older sons with Benjamin, the youngest in his brood of boys.

⏳ *Is there someone you have a difficult time trusting?*

⏳ *Does a person have to be perfect for you to trust him or her?*

⏳ *What does it mean to trust someone?*

⏳ *Is it possible to forgive someone without trust being restored?*

> **So the sons of Israel came to buy grain among those who were coming, for the famine was in the land of Canaan also.**
>
> **Now Joseph was the ruler over the land; he was the one who sold to all the people of the land. And Joseph's brothers came and bowed down to him with their faces to the ground. (Genesis 42:5–6)**

Before we read any further in the story of Joseph, let's remind ourselves of one of the dreams Joseph had when he was a mere teenager.

> **He said to them, "Please listen to this dream which I have had; for behold, we were binding sheaves in the field, and lo, my sheaf rose up and also stood erect; and behold, your sheaves gathered around and bowed down to my sheaf." (Genesis 37:6–7)**

The ten sons of Jacob had not yet realized that the ruler in Egypt was their younger brother; they just knew that they were in acute need of food for their families. When they came to ask for assistance, they respectfully and appropriately bowed their faces to the ground. They bowed out of respect for his position. This is the precise scenario Joseph prophesied as just a young lad through the dream given to him by God.

Who Is This Man?

Although Joseph instantly recognized this gang of former delinquents as his brothers, he treated them as strangers and aliens. He spoke to them authoritatively and powerfully as one would expect from a man in his position.

> *When Joseph saw his brothers he recognized them, but he disguised himself to them and spoke to them harshly. And he said to them, "Where have you come from?" And they said, "From the land of Canaan, to buy food."*
>
> *But Joseph had recognized his brothers, although they did not recognize him.*
> **(Genesis 42:7–8)**

There are many reasons why these ten men did not recognize their younger brother Joseph. First of all, they probably assumed he was dead. Also, he looked and spoke like an Egyptian officer. He was clean-shaven and used Egyptian language—they were from Canaan and likely spoke Hebrew. Joseph also wore the trappings of Egyptian royalty and now used an Egyptian name. There was nothing about Joseph's outward appearance that would remind them of the young man who was their long-lost brother.

> *Joseph remembered the dreams which he had about them, and said to them, "You are spies; you have come to look at the undefended parts of our land." Then they said to him, "No, my lord, but your servants have come to buy food. We are all sons of one man; we are honest men, your servants are not spies."*
> **(Genesis 42:9–11)**

I wonder if Joseph wanted to unceremoniously charge out of the room when he heard their vapid response. When they said, "We are honest men," Joseph likely felt sick to his royal stomach.

Three items in this conversation are truisms spoken by Joseph's brothers:

1. We have come to buy food.
2. We are sons of one man.
3. We are not spies.

However, their statement, "We are honest men," was a serious lie and likely set off alarms in Joseph's heart.

A Test

Joseph's serious and authoritative behavior was necessary because he needed to test his brothers to discern if they were the same mean-spirited, obnoxious, pig-headed young men from two decades before. Joseph vitally needed to know if they had matured into honest men and if their hearts had softened at all.

> But they said, "Your servants are twelve brothers in all, the sons of one man in the land of Canaan; and behold, the youngest is with our father today, and one is no longer alive." Joseph said to them, "It is as I said to you, you are spies; by this you will be tested: by the life of Pharaoh, you shall not go from this place unless your youngest brother comes here! Send one of you that he may get your brother, while you remain confined, that your words may be tested, whether there is truth in you. But if not, by the life of Pharaoh, surely you are spies." So he put them all together in prison for three days. (Genesis 42:13–17)

⧗ *Do you believe it was necessary for Joseph to test his brothers? Why or why not?*

⧗ *When someone has betrayed you, it is important to forgive, but trust is a different response than forgiveness. Should you immediately trust the person who betrayed you or does trust take time?*

> Now Joseph said to them on the third day, "Do this and live, for I fear God." (Genesis 42:18)

After three days, Joseph removed his brothers from prison because he feared God and desired to follow His ways. Joseph knew he must allow his brothers the freedom they had denied him. I also believe Joseph remembered the stark cruelty of his brothers from decades before. But because of his relationship with God, his eternal and compassionate Father, he refused to act as a man of revenge.

> If you are honest men, let one of your brothers be confined in your prison; but as for the rest of you, go, carry grain for the famine of your households, and bring your

youngest brother to me, so your words may be verified, and you will not die." And they did so. (Genesis 42:19–20)

⧖ Aren't you thankful you serve a God who fills you with joy and peace? Read the treasure verse for the week and allow it to encourage you no matter what you are going through.

If you know that God loves you, you should never question a directive from Him. It will always be right and best. When He gives you a directive, you are not just to observe it, discuss it, or debate it. You are to obey it.

— Henry Blackaby
On Mission with God

Day 4

Heartbreaking, Indeed

In the ensuing conversation, after Joseph had released his brothers from a three-day prison stay and informed them of his decision, we are given a heartbreaking tidbit of information. The brothers are still in the presence of Joseph and, although they don't recognize him, he knows exactly who they are.

Joseph instructed his ten brothers that nine of them were free to go and take grain with them; however, one brother would stay as collateral. He ordered them to bring their youngest brother back to Egypt. Joseph cautioned his siblings that this was the only way he would trust them. The nine eldest sons of Jacob's family then began to discuss, in their own language, their concerns about the conundrum. This lets us, the readers, in on an excruciating secret. As a young man in the pit, Joseph desperately begged for his life and was ignored by his brothers.

> *Then they said to one another, "Truly we are guilty concerning our brother, because we saw the distress of his soul when he pleaded with us, yet we would not listen; therefore this distress has come upon us." Reuben answered them, saying, "Did I not tell you, 'Do not sin against the boy'; and you would not listen? Now comes the reckoning for his blood."* (Genesis 42:21–22)

Sowing and Reaping

Even though decades had passed since their mistreatment of Joseph, the brothers immediately recognized their sin as the catalyst for what was about to transpire. The law of "sowing and reaping" is seen through Scripture from its beginning to its end. These guilty men knew what they had sown more than twenty years before and believed they would now reap those devastating consequences.

Would you be interested enough to read a long quote by a great theologian and scholar of the last century? I hope you will absorb the words that F. B. Meyer wrote so long ago about this part of Scripture. It will cause you to groan, weep, and examine your own heart.

"Year passed year; but the years could not obliterate from their memories that look, those cries, that scene in the green glen of Dothan, surrounded by the tall cliffs, over-arched by the blue sky, whose expanse was lit up by a meridian sun. They tried to lock up the skeleton in their most secret cupboard, but it contrived to come forth to confront them. . . . Sometimes they thought they saw that agonized young face in their dreams, and heard that piteous voice wailing in the night wind. . . . One crime may thus darken a whole life. There are some who teach that God is too merciful to punish men; yet He has so made the world that sin is its own Nemesis—sin carries with it the seed of its own punishment. And the men who carry with them the sense of unforgiven sin will be the first to believe in a vulture forever tearing out the vitals, a worm that never dies, fire that is never quenched."[18]

Do not be deceived, God is not mocked; for whatever a man sows, this he will also reap. (Galatians 6:7)

The biblical passage above, penned by Paul through the urging of the Holy Spirit, thousands of years after the life of Joseph, serves as a sobering yet vital reminder. The seeds we plant today bear the harvest of our life tomorrow. Often this Scripture is quoted in correlation with financial giving, but it also can be applied to other areas of life such as these:

- If you need a friend—be a friend.
- If you need prayer—pray for someone else.
- If you long to be a mother—work in the church nursery.
- If you are lonely—encourage someone in need of encouragement.

⏳ *What is the greatest need in your life right now?*

⏳ *How can you "sow" in order to "reap" in this area?*

Haunted by Sin

We find a piece of information in Genesis 42:21–22 that was previously hidden in the story of Joseph. His terrified brothers were having a private conversation and nervously referenced the heartbreaking fact that Joseph pled for his life. He begged his brothers not to leave him, not to beat him up, and not to throw him in the pit. However, the hard-hearted brothers ignored his cries for help and Joseph's lonely and futile supplications had haunted them for more than two decades. Their sin stayed buried deep within their emotional framework and refused to abate.

Is there a sin from the past you need to be released from today? All it takes is whispering a heartfelt prayer of confession and then asking Jesus to forgive you. You can walk in the freedom and forgiveness Joseph's brothers ignored. Perhaps you need to ask a person to forgive you for the pain you caused them. Confession, forgiveness, and freedom are all a beautiful part of God's spiritual equation for our lives. When you humble yourself and admit your wrongdoings you experience rich and enormous freedom.

The Sad Saga Continues . . .

As Joseph's ten older brothers discussed their strategy, they were unaware that Joseph could understand every word they said. They assumed he was Egyptian and had no idea he understood Hebrew.

> *They did not know, however, that Joseph understood, for there was an interpreter between them. He turned away from them and wept. But when he returned to them and spoke to them, he took Simeon from them and bound him before their eyes.* **(Genesis 42:23–24)**

While Joseph listened to their words, all the pain of the past two decades rushed across his weary heart. This was his family. The same blood flowed through their veins, they shared the same prominent Jewish noses, similar physical features, and the same earthly father. Despite their many similarities, the differences caused a painful and extensive meanwhile in all of their lives.

⧗ *What are some similarities you share with your family members?*

⧗ *What are some differences?*

⏳ *How does your family handle its differences?*

> **Then Joseph gave orders to fill their bags with grain and to restore every man's money in his sack, and to give them provisions for the journey. And thus it was done for them.**
>
> **So they loaded their donkeys with their grain and departed from there. As one of them opened his sack to give his donkey fodder at the lodging place, he saw his money; and behold, it was in the mouth of his sack. Then he said to his brothers, "My money has been returned, and behold, it is even in my sack." And their hearts sank, and they turned trembling to one another, saying, "What is this that God has done to us?"** (Genesis 42:25–28)

I must admit, as I studied that final sentence in this passage, "What is this that God has done to us?" I shook my head with a sad but knowing smile on my face. These men now blamed God for the situation they were in. However, I must also admit, I have often blamed God for unfairness, for a horrible situation of my own making, and for terrible circumstances. What I was unable to see in those moments of confusion was that God was really working all things together for my good and for His glory.

I must remind myself, especially when I am crushed by human experiences as a believer in Christ, not to blame God. Instead, I should bless God. I must never allow my formidable situation to turn my heart away from God's goodness and His true character.

⏳ *How does the phrase, "Don't blame God—bless Him!" shift your perspective as you deal with troubling events in life?*

Joseph's brothers were confused yet they were given abundant provisions. They were distraught and yet they received their money back. They had numerous questions and yet carried grain with which to feed their families. These nine tortured souls were on the road back home, yet they wondered if they would live or die.

Joseph was in the palace, possibly wondering if he had seen the last of his brothers or if they would come back for Simeon. Perhaps he wondered if they would actually bring Benjamin to Egypt or not. And his battered heart surely ached to see his elderly father once again.

Life is never easy, is it? What a tangled web Joseph's family had woven. But remember, we have historical perspective. We know the end of the story and it's a fabulous one.

⧗ *I hope you are enjoying your treasure verse this week. It is one of my favorites and fortifies my soul every time I read it.*

Nothing is a surprise to God; nothing is a setback to His plans;
nothing can thwart His purposes; and nothing is beyond His control.
His sovereignty is absolute. Everything that happens is uniquely ordained by God.
Sovereignty is a weighty thing to ascribe to the nature and character of God.
Yet if He were not sovereign, He would not be God.
The Bible is clear that God is in control of everything that happens.

—Joni Eareckson Tada
When God Weeps

Day 5

A Mountain of Events

When Joseph's brothers returned to the family homestead in Canaan, although they brought provisions, they did not bring good news for their aging father.

> *When they came to their father Jacob in the land of Canaan, they told him all that had happened to them, saying, 'The man, the lord of the land, spoke harshly with us, and took us for spies of the country. But we said to him, 'We are honest men; we are not spies. We are twelve brothers, sons of our father; one is no longer alive, and the youngest is with our father today in the land of Canaan.' 'The man, the lord of the land, said to us, 'By this I will know that you are honest men: leave one of your brothers with me and take grain for the famine of your households, and go. But bring your youngest brother to me that I may know that you are not spies, but honest men. I will give your brother to you, and you may trade in the land.' "*
>
> *Now it came about as they were emptying their sacks, that behold, every man's bundle of money was in his sack; and when they and their father saw their bundles of money, they were dismayed. Their father Jacob said to them, "You have bereaved me of my children: Joseph is no more, and Simeon is no more, and you would take Benjamin; all these things are against me." Then Reuben spoke to his father, saying, "You may put my two sons to death if I do not bring him back to you; put him in my care, and I will return him to you." But Jacob said, "My son shall not go down with you; for his brother is dead, and he alone is left. If harm should befall him on the journey you are taking, then you will bring my gray hair down to Sheol in sorrow."*
> (Genesis 42:29–38)

Jacob roared at his sons with incredulity at their request. He refused to allow Benjamin to go to Egypt with them knowing he was unable to trust their protection or decision-making. Jacob was not about to lose yet another child because of his other children's lack of wisdom.

⏳ *What issues in life make you angry?*

⧗   *When you are angry with the people you love, how do you act toward them?*

⧗   *What is an appropriate response for a Christian who is dealing with an anger-stirred situation?*

Once Upon a Time

The events of Genesis 43 grow in intensity as we draw closer to the day of restoration for Joseph's family. I hope you will take the time to read it in its entirety, but I will share with you, in my own words, the overview of this chapter.

The famine grew more severe and once again, Jacob's family ran out of food. To avoid starvation, Jacob told his sons they had no choice but to return to Egypt. But this time Judah spoke up. He reminded his father that they couldn't go back without taking Benjamin with them. After a long discussion, Jacob finally relented and agreed to allow his youngest son to accompany his older brothers, in hopes they would return with Benjamin, but also with Simeon. To sweeten the deal, Jacob also sent gifts to the difficult man in charge of the Egyptian food supply. He sent balm, honey, aromatic gum, myrrh, pistachios, and almonds. Jacob also returned the money that was in their sacks and sent twice the financial payment he had last time. As his sons departed, some biblical translations quote Jacob's final words as, "If my sons die . . . they die."

When the brothers arrived in Egypt once again, Joseph took one look at Benjamin's sweet face and prepared a sumptuous feast. He invited all of Jacob's sons to dine with him. The older brothers nervously informed Joseph that they had discovered the money in their sacks and had brought it to him, as well as twice the payment that was expected for grain.

The Response of a Leader

Joseph may be the premiere biblical example of a godly leader. He gives glory to God in every situation and in every conversation. Leadership is not so much about being in charge as it is about taking care of the people under your charge. A godly leader lives with an awareness of the Lord's guidance in matters both great and small.

> *He said, "Be at ease, do not be afraid. Your God and the God of your father has given*
> *you treasure in your sacks; I had your money." Then he brought Simeon out to them.*
> **(Genesis 43:23)**

This event in ancient Scripture reminds me of a New Testament verse that serves as a reminder of how God chooses to pursue all those who are caught in sin.

Or do you think lightly of the riches of His kindness and tolerance and patience,
not knowing that the kindness of God leads you to repentance?

—Romans 2:4

Joseph was kind to his brothers, and this will remain part of their story of repentance. God is kind to all those who have rejected Him because it is His kindness that pursues and draws us.

> *Then the man brought the men into Joseph's house and gave them water, and they*
> *washed their feet; and he gave their donkeys fodder. So they prepared the present*
> *for Joseph's coming at noon; for they had heard that they were to eat a meal there.*
> *When Joseph came home, they brought into the house to him the present*
> *which was in their hand and bowed to the ground before him. Then he asked them*
> *about their welfare, and said, "Is your old father well, of whom you spoke? Is he*
> *still alive?" They said, "Your servant our father is well; he is still alive." They*
> *bowed down in homage. As he lifted his eyes and saw his brother Benjamin, his*
> *mother's son, he said, "Is this your youngest brother, of whom you spoke to me?"*
> *And he said, "May God be gracious to you, my son." (Genesis 43:24–29)*

Can't you just hear the longing in Joseph's voice? Doesn't your heart ache for this man who has lived for more than twenty years knowing his brothers despised him? It must have been overwhelmingly bittersweet for Joseph to once again be with his siblings, yet knowing he had missed so much of their lives.

I hope you will apply these reunion verses of the family of Jacob to your broken relationship situation. This is a picture of promise and blessing for those of you whose families have fractured because of sin, dysfunction, and misunderstanding. God is more than able to restore the most fragmented of families. Joseph remained a person of honor and integrity through all the years of separation from his kinsmen, knowing God was with him during the long days when they were not.

You can be sure God was listening to the words that came out of Joseph's mouth. He is also listening to the words that come out of yours. If God was able to restore the family of Joseph, He is able to do it again in the family that you hold so dear.

⧗   *Do you have a sad separation issue in your family? Or perhaps someone you know is dealing with this type of division. Can you think of a scripture with wisdom for this type of family alienation?*

The Heart of Joseph

I am simply and completely undone by this ancient story. Tears are cascading down my cheeks as I join in both the regretful mourning and sweet joy exploding in Joseph's heart.

> **Joseph hurried out for he was deeply stirred over his brother, and he sought a place to weep; and he entered his chamber and wept there. Then he washed his face and came out; and he controlled himself and said, "Serve the meal." (Genesis 43:30–31)**

Was Joseph about to experience the moment he had longed for or the moment he had dreaded?

> **So they served him by himself, and them by themselves, and the Egyptians who ate with him by themselves, because the Egyptians could not eat bread with the Hebrews, for that is loathsome to the Egyptians. Now they were seated before him, the firstborn according to his birthright and the youngest according to his youth, and the men looked at one another in astonishment. He took portions to them from his own table, but Benjamin's portion was five times as much as any of theirs. So they feasted and drank freely with him. (Genesis 43:32–34)**

Due to Egyptian protocol, Joseph's brothers ate in the same room with him but not at the same table. I wonder if the mystified brothers were astonished that Joseph could place them in exact birth order but still the light of recognition had not dawned in their balding heads. Joseph showed immense favor to the youngest brother, Benjamin. This should have revealed so much more than a meal with strangers. It held the potential of a long-awaited family reunion.

To Be Continued

Again, I ask you to read another chapter in Genesis, this time 44, in its entirety. But for now, I'll recap it for you in my words.

All eleven brothers, from oldest to youngest, were sent on their way the next morning. Joseph, however, had once again placed money in each man's sack. But this time, in Benjamin's, he planted his own silver cup. Following their departure, Joseph sent his servant on their trail to confront them about what was in their sacks—particularly highlighting the missing cup. The men were stunned at the accusation of the servant. They reminded him that they had already returned the money discovered the last time they left Egypt and knew nothing of a silver cup. So completely convinced were they of each other's innocence, they told the servant, "If you find the cup in one of our sacks, you can kill the thief and the rest of us will stay in Egypt as your slaves."

The servant ripped into each parcel in the possession of this parade of eleven brothers. He started with the sack of the eldest and went in descending birth order. The tension must have hung heavy. Surely, they looked at one another with silent hope yet desperation. As each sequential sack proved void of the missing silver cup, they all must have breathed a collective sigh of relief. Finally, only one sack remained for examination—Benjamin's, the youngest of them all.

> *He searched, beginning with the oldest and ending with the youngest, and the cup was found in Benjamin's sack. Then they tore their clothes, and when each man loaded his donkey, they returned to the city.* **(Genesis 44:12–13)**

They had torn Joseph's robe many years ago and now they tore their own. It was inconceivable that this was happening to them. They reloaded their possessions and mournfully and quietly returned to Egypt to face the royal palace and the man in charge.

> *When Judah and his brothers came to Joseph's house, he was still there, and they fell to the ground before him.* **(Genesis 44:14)**

Joseph's brothers once again lay prostrate at the feet of their brother, Joseph. They were at his mercy. The prophetic dream came to pass in the lives of this interesting, ruptured family. But there is more to come—something fantastic and nearly unbelievable. And I can assure you that no matter what you are going through today, God has fantastic things in store for you, as well. In your meanwhile, God is working out all the details, all the brokenness, and all the disappointment together for a greater good. It's a promise.

⌛ *Have you finished memorizing your treasure verse yet?*

*Faith is deliberate confidence in the character
of God Whose ways you cannot understand
at the time.*

—Oswald Chambers

THE JOSEPH PRINCIPLE

Elisabeth Howard Elliot

Elisabeth Howard was born on December 27, 1926, in Brussels, Belgium, where her parents served as missionaries. Before she was a year old, they moved to Germantown, Pennsylvania. In America, Elisabeth gained four younger brothers and one little sister.

The Howard home may have run like a military compound, but it was also lovingly filled to overflowing with hymns and scriptures and missionaries-on-furlough. Elisabeth sat at the dinner table with the likes of Betty Stam, whose later martyrdom deeply impacted her life and her call. Elisabeth grew tall and slender, a thinking introvert, with a sharp mind and tenacious stubbornness. Someday, she would need these qualities for the unusual work God had in store for her.

A true female pioneer in the world of conservative Christianity, Elisabeth went to Wheaton College and studied Greek. She believed her life's calling was to translate the Bible for the remote regions in the world. While at college, she met a dashing young man, Jim Elliot, also called to the mission field. After graduation, Elisabeth went on a missionary expedition to Ecuador with other students from Wheaton, including Jim.

In the first year of their trip, Jim and Elisabeth worked in different regions. In 1953, Jim and Elisabeth were married and continued to serve in Ecuador together. Their daughter, Valerie, was born there.

Jim and his fellow missionaries believed God had called them to the Auca tribe and were strategic, prayerful, and bold in their approach. However, on January 8, 1956, after flying their small plane to the beach close to this tribe, all five missionaries were murdered.

When the Auca tribe in Eastern Ecuador killed Jim Elliot and his missionary partners, it thrust Elisabeth into a world of both grief and fame.

As a new widow with a toddler, Elisabeth unbelievably moved in with the fierce tribe that killed her husband, longing to show them the love of Christ. This single act became the most celebrated (and criticized) of her life, but a closer look at her story reveals that most of Elisabeth's time on the field was anything but notable. Her years as a missionary can rather be described as confusing, stark, and tumultuous.

While residing with the Quichua tribe for a year, two Auca women shared quarters with Elisabeth. During that time, Elisabeth learned why the tribe killed her husband and the other missionaries. With that understanding, Elisabeth was able to go to the Auca tribe and build relationships with them. She helped lead the people of the tribe to Jesus.

After spending two years with the Auca, Elisabeth and Valerie returned to America in 1963 and lived in the northeast. It was there Elisabeth met Addison Leitch, a theologian professor at Gordon Conwell University. They were happily married in 1969.

Four years after they were married, in 1973, Addison lost his battle with cancer and died.

After Leitch's death, Elisabeth then opened her Massachusetts home to lodgers. During the next few years, she had two lodgers, one of whom married her daughter, and the other lodger, Lars Gren, married Elisabeth. Lars and Elisabeth were married until her death.

Elisabeth Elliot once asked philosophically, "Would you like to have the story of Daniel without the lions' den? . . . Would you like to have the story of Joseph without all his trials and tribulations, without his going into the pit?"[19]

Elliot had the wisdom and experience to pose such questions because her own story was filled with lions' dens and dark pits.

But her sufferings were never intended to be her defining moment. The *manner* in which she suffered makes her a sterling role model. Her steady trust with an enthusiastic hope in a good God who makes no mistakes carried her through. She wrote:

> It depends on our willingness to see everything in God, receive all from His hand, accept with gratitude just the portion and the cup He offers. Shall I charge Him with a mistake in His measurements or with misjudging the sphere in which I can best learn to trust Him? Has He misplaced me? Is He ignorant of things or people which, in my view, hinder my doing His will?
>
> . . . The secret is *Christ* in *me*, not me in a different set of circumstances.[20]

While Elliot is best known for her husband's martyrdom and her courageous ministry to the Waodanis, biographer Ellen Vaughn writes that "her most noble accomplishment was not weathering that excoriating loss [of her husband Jim]. It was practicing—through both the high dramas and the low, dull days that constitute any human life—the daily self-death required for one's soul to flourish."[21]

Early in life, Elisabeth resolved to obey God no matter what—not just in the prominent moments, but also in the prosaic and banal. Whether speaking to a maid or waitress or speaking to rapt audiences, she embraced the uneventful moments of daily life over Christian celebrity. For Elisabeth, the scholar, the missionary, the widow, and the mother, "the only measure of any human action came down to one thing: obedience."[22] Elisabeth Elliot's story is a remarkable one, not because of her celebrated successes or sufferings, but because she fixed her eyes on Jesus, the Author and Finisher of her faith. She loved Him above all else and obeyed Him without a thought for comfort or selfish pleasures. Jesus was her Lord and trusted Savior through the lions' dens and the dark pits until she passed through the gates of splendor in 2015.

Elliot's life models for us a compelling faith that causes us to ask ourselves, *How can I lovingly lay down my life, despite great weakness and tribulation and tedium, so the gospel reaches the farthest corners of the world?*

It is God to whom and with whom we travel, and while
He is the end of our journey, He is also at every stopping place.

— Elisabeth Elliot

Week 8

Only God!

Day 1

They Passed the Test

I suppose we are all waiting for something to change in our lives, aren't we? We hope, pray, and believe for adverse conditions to transform through a miracle, knowing that is exactly what it will take.

One of the grandest lessons I have learned from the life of Joseph is about perspective. What I see happening in natural circumstances is not all that is taking place. God is moving, working, and strategizing in the unseen world to perform a great and lasting goodness through my uncomfortable situations.

Gut-Wrenching Grief

We left Joseph's brothers on their faces in front of Joseph, second in command in all of Egypt. These overgrown boys were in a dire predicament. Joseph's silver cup was found in Benjamin's sack. Benjamin, the youngest of the twelve brothers, was dearly loved by Jacob, their father, and even more so since Joseph's disappearance and reported death.

> *Joseph said to them, "What is this deed that you have done? Do you not know that such a man as I can indeed practice divination?" So Judah said, "What can we say to my lord? What can we speak? And how can we justify ourselves? God has found out the iniquity of your servants; behold, we are my lord's slaves, both we and the one in whose possession the cup has been found." But he said, "Far be it from me to do this. The man in whose possession the cup has been found, he shall be my slave; but as for you, go up in peace to your father." (Genesis 44:15–17)*

Joseph's brothers explained the situation to him with great angst. They even torn their clothes asunder, so intense was their emotional pain. They must have moaned and heaved as they told Joseph how precious Benjamin was to their father, especially since the death of their other brother many years earlier. Little did these emotionally charged men know they were talking to the deceased, who was alive and well and in charge.

A Heart of Compassion

> *Then Judah approached him, and said, "Oh my lord, may your servant please speak a word in my lord's ears, and do not be angry with your servant; for you are equal to Pharaoh. My lord asked his servants, saying, 'Have you a father or a brother?'*
>
> *We said to my lord, 'We have an old father and a little child of his old age. Now his brother is dead, so he alone is left of his mother, and his father loves him.' Then you said to your servants, 'Bring him down to me that I may set my eyes on him.' But we said to my lord, 'The lad cannot leave his father, for if he should leave his father, his father would die.' You said to your servants, however, 'Unless your youngest brother comes down with you, you will not see my face again.' Thus it came about when we went up to your servant my father, we told him the words of my lord. Our father said, 'Go back, buy us a little food.' But we said, 'We cannot go down. If our youngest brother is with us, then we will go down; for we cannot see the man's face unless our youngest brother is with us.' Your servant my father said to us, 'You know that my wife bore me two sons; and the one went out from me, and I said, "Surely he is torn in pieces," and I have not seen him since. If you take this one also from me, and harm befalls him, you will bring my gray hair down to Sheol in sorrow."* (Genesis 44:18–29)

Judah became the spokesperson and implored Joseph to allow Benjamin to go home to their father. He offered his own life in exchange for Benjamin's, knowing Benjamin's death would kill their father. Bible theologians and scholars have recognized Judah's plea as "the most moving address in the Word of God."[23]

> *Now, therefore, when I come to your servant my father, and the lad is not with us, since his life is bound up in the lad's life, when he sees that the lad is not with us, he will die. Thus your servants will bring the gray hair of your servant our father down to Sheol in sorrow. For your servant became surety for the lad to my father, saying, "If I do not bring him back to you, then let me bear the blame before my father forever." Now, therefore, please let your servant remain instead of the lad a slave to my lord, and let the lad go up with his brothers. For how shall I go up to my father if the lad is not with me—for fear that I see the evil that would overtake my father?* (Genesis 44:30–34)

⧗   *How have your feelings changed toward these brothers?*

⧗   *How do you think Benjamin is responding to the emotion and pain since he likely knows nothing of how the brothers had treated Joseph?*

⧗   *What adjective would you use to describe Judah at this point in the story?*

People Can Change

Before we view one more scene from this thrilling and sobering narrative, remember that Joseph has been testing his brothers since their first trip to Egypt. He deeply desired to investigate their hearts to see if they had changed or not. One of the miracles we see unfolding in Joseph's meanwhile is that his brothers had indeed been transformed. They told the truth at every juncture, they took responsibility for the situation, and they honored their father.

⧗   *Have you ever observed a dynamic change in the life of someone?*

⧗   *What instigated this change?*

⧗   *Do you believe it is possible to make a radical change in one's life without the help and strength of the Lord?*

A Cry Heard Throughout the Palace

Doesn't it just make you weep? The Holy Spirit has given us an extraordinary view into the broken heart that Joseph endured all the years of his meanwhile.

> *Then Joseph could not control himself before all those who stood by him, and he cried, "Have everyone go out from me." So there was no man with him when Joseph made himself known to his brothers. He wept so loudly that the Egyptians heard it, and the household of Pharaoh heard of it.* (Genesis 45:1–2)

Joseph was out of control. His emotions were running down his handsome cheeks. His well-honed chest heaved with years of rejection. Joseph was crying so loudly the entire household heard him as his sobs pierced the royal atmosphere. The palace was a massive structure but the sound of Joseph's pain efficiently traveled down the halls, carried along the cold marble walls and stone floors. The cries of Joseph echoed through every chamber and into every room. I believe Joseph's cries reached the Throne Room of God as well.

As we bring this portion of the story to a close, I can't help but remember a verse that has meant so much to me over some excruciatingly painful times in my life.

> *The Lord is near to the brokenhearted And saves those who are crushed in spirit.*
>
> *—Psalm 34:18*

Perhaps the reason Joseph had such an authentic awareness of the Lord's presence was because he had a broken, ravaged heart. Joseph knew the Lord was hovering close to him, watching him, and taking care of him. If your heart is broken, I pray you too know, like Joseph did, that the Lord is with you.

⧗   *Why is it vital for you to know, as a believer in Christ, that He is near you when you have a broken heart?*

Hidden Treasure: Read this verse out loud several times today and write it out on a 3x5 card. Think about this verse throughout the week and begin to commit it to memory:

I love the Lord, because He hears My voice and my supplications.
Because He has inclined His ear to me, Therefore
I shall call upon Him as long as I live.

—Psalm 116:1–2

We want to avoid suffering, death, sin, ashes. But we live
in a world crushed and broken and torn, a world God
Himself visited to redeem. We receive His poured-out life,
and being allowed the high privilege of suffering with Him,
may then pour ourselves out for others.

—Elisabeth Elliot
A Lamp Unto My Feet

Day 2

The "Wow" Factor

I am emotionally drained, and we haven't even reached the conclusion of this ancient chronicle yet. I am haunted by Joseph's cries bouncing off the walls of the palace while his staff scurried to figure out what was wrong. And can you imagine his brothers? They were likely heartsick as the events of their past life rolled through their minds. Were they even standing on their feet? Had they fallen to their knees in shock and emotional torture?

> *Then Joseph could not control himself before all those who stood by him, and he cried, "Have everyone go out from me." So there was no man with him when Joseph made himself known to his brothers. He wept so loudly that the Egyptians heard it, and the household of Pharaoh heard of it. Then Joseph said to his brothers, "I am Joseph! Is my father still alive?" But his brothers could not answer him, for they were dismayed at his presence. (Genesis 45:1–3)*

"I am Joseph!" Those three words ricochet down through the centuries and we, as the readers and students of this unbelievable story, know we have reached the climax of the meanwhile for this family. There are few more dramatic and fulfilling moments than this in all recorded history.

"I am!" This part of Joseph's cry holds deep meaning. "I am!" was the reminder of God to Moses at the burning bush (Exodus 3). "I am!" said Jesus to His disciples in the middle of the storm (Matthew 14:27).

When Joseph informed his brothers of his true identity, they were rendered speechless. The word *dismayed* in verse 3 is the Hebrew word *bahal* and it literally means terrified. All of the brothers' worst-case scenarios now flooded their minds as they imagined what Joseph could do to them. Joseph was the power broker in the situation and thus far he appeared very stern and unyielding.

I imagine the brothers, except Benjamin, were aware that Joseph could kill them, lock them in prison, and seek revenge for what they had done to him. The brotherhood held no power in this formidable situation. They only had regret, shame, and fear.

⧗　*Are you the type of person who imagines worst-case scenarios?*

⧗　*Why does the Bible tell us at least 365 times "don't be afraid"?*

Draw Close

Ultimately, Joseph begged his brothers to draw close to him. I believe he was not only inviting a physical closeness in the moment, but an emotional nearness in the years to come.

> **Then Joseph said to his brothers, "Please come closer to me." And they came closer. And he said, "I am your brother Joseph, whom you sold into Egypt." (Genesis 45:4)**

Decades of alienation were gloriously over for the sons of Jacob. Now, it was time for unbridled joy and sweet fellowship—their meanwhile suddenly behind them. I imagine Joseph gathered them all in a hug and looked into their faces as he grinned in recognition of who they had become.

"Judah! Your wife must be a good cook. It shows!"

"Asher, brother, where did all of your hair go?"

"Dan, how many children do you have?"

"Simeon, remember the time we climbed the tree and couldn't get down?"

⧗　*What can you do today to restore a broken relationship? Whether it's a family member or a friend, what can you say or how can you act in a practical sense, to restore dignity to the relationship?*

The Plan of God

You might want to get a tissue before we read the next verse together. In this passage, the "wow" of Joseph's story begins.

> **"Now do not be grieved or angry with yourselves, because you sold me here, for God sent me before you to preserve life." (Genesis 45:5)**

Joseph, in that one sentence, removed years of blame and shame from their lives. His words were so generous and compassionate that regret and pain surely fled instantly from all ten broken hearts. Joseph was so convinced of the consuming, restorative, and powerful plan of God that he immediately informed his brothers he held absolutely nothing against them. There was not one shred of blame or unforgiveness in Joseph's tone. Joseph was wisely aware that the hand of providence was more significant and pervasive than any minor act of a mere human being. God's plans are bigger than our meanwhiles. God's will for our individual lives is greater than a moment of discomfort.

⧗   *Can you make a similar declaration over the pain of your past? Write it out below.*

Joseph was more aware of the plan of God than he was of the rejection he had experienced. Joseph knew his words would set the tone for the relationship with his brothers for years to come. He spoke kindly, compassionately, and even sacredly. Joseph transformed the ugliness of their rift by demonstrating the heart of the Father toward His children. Joseph had the wisdom to turn the scathing into something sacred.

We live in a kingdom often described as "upside down." Today's pop psychology would have advised Joseph to vent his true feelings and repeat the unfair and extreme impact from his brothers' treatment. A secular counselor might have recommended Joseph send his brothers away and tell them to never come back again. But the world's way has never been God's way.

Joseph's words are a challenge to me personally. When I am met with someone who has offended me, used me, or even bullied me, I must recognize that God was with me in my days of deepest pain. I must focus on the amazing work God has done in my heart and in my life. I simply must.

Examining Joseph as a son, brother, servant, prisoner, and now as a leader, I believe the most distinguishing feature of his life was his desire to turn every conversation to the Lord whom He served. Nearly every sentence Joseph speaks throughout his years, as recorded in the Bible, has the name of God in it. Oh! How I long to bring the name of my Lord into every conversation in which I engage.

⧗   *What do you see as the most distinguishing feature of Joseph's life?*

A True Leader

We are about to listen to the words of a true leader. An influencer so great and compelling that his words echo through the canyons of time. Joseph spoke generously because his life had been refined by human pain and he saw the unprecedented and miraculous plan of God unfold.

> *For the famine has been in the land these two years, and there are still five years in which there will be neither plowing nor harvesting. God sent me before you to preserve for you a remnant in the earth, and to keep you alive by a great deliverance. Now, therefore, it was not you who sent me here, but God; and He has made me a father to Pharaoh and lord of all his household and ruler over all the land of Egypt.* (Genesis 45:6–8)

⧖   *Make a list of some of the leadership traits you have seen in Joseph.*

Don't miss this small phrase hidden away in this trio of verses. "He has made me a father to Pharaoh." Undoubtedly, the Pharaoh of that time was older than Joseph biologically, and yet, Joseph had developed a unique relationship with him. The Hebrew word Joseph used to describe his relationship with the highest ruler in the land is *ab* and it means the head of an individual or household, protector or one who is respected or honored. The roles had reversed between Joseph and Pharaoh. Joseph was the one Pharaoh turned to for wisdom, insight, and guidance. Joseph's brothers refused his leadership when he was a young man, but Pharaoh embraced it.

The life and words of Joseph serve as a stirring reminder that God's will is the controlling reality of every event in our broken lives. Man's shortcomings bow to the will and ways of God. Human disappointment falls on its face and is transformed in His presence. When you truly know God is with you, you can sense the hand of God upon your life. When you are more aware of His presence than you are of your own misery, you are able to fully and completely forgive those who have wronged you.

Human error never has the last word—God does. Devastation never rules and reigns supreme—God does. Family pain never casts the deciding vote—God does. Sin never wins—God does.

Regardless of what has transpired over the years, the God of Joseph is the God of you. His goodness will write the closing chapter of your story.

⧗ *Turn your treasure verse this week into a prayer.*

Towards himself a Christian should have a broken spirit, but towards God it should be one of rejoicing always in Him. He rejoices not for its own sake nor because of any joyful experience, work, blessing or circumstance, but exclusively because God is his center.

—Watchman Nee
Journeying Towards the Spiritual

Day 3

The Reunion

Joseph couldn't wait to see his beloved father, Jacob, once again. In the sheer joy of the family reunion among the brothers, there was only one thing missing and that was their patriarch.

> *Hurry and go up to my father, and say to him, "Thus says your son Joseph, 'God has made me lord of all Egypt; come down to me, do not delay. You shall live in the land of Goshen, and you shall be near me, you and your children and your children's children and your flocks and your herds and all that you have. There I will also provide for you, for there are still five years of famine to come, and you and your household and all that you have would be impoverished.' " Behold, your eyes see, and the eyes of my brother Benjamin see, that it is my mouth which is speaking to you.* (Genesis 45:9–12)

Joseph assured his brothers there would always be a place for his large family with him. Joseph was willing to provide for them and honor them. Joseph's words of love and compassion were followed by actions. Joseph not only forgave verbally, but he also forgave with his heart and in deeds. Joseph dignified those who had wronged him with a practical and powerful blessing.

⌛ *Ask the Lord to show you how you can bless someone who has betrayed you in the past.*

Your life was not meant to be a receptacle of hoarded blessings or of stifled compassion. I would rather err on the side of too much forgiveness, abundant mercy, and lavish love, than restrain my ability to exhibit God's love to others.

When We All Get to Heaven

What happens next in this saga of hope and reconciliation is a foreshadowing of what you and I will experience when we leave time and walk into eternity. (You might want to make sure you have a box of tissues close by as we continue to rejoice with Joseph.)

> *Then he fell on his brother Benjamin's neck and wept, and Benjamin wept on his neck. He kissed all his brothers and wept on them, and afterward his brothers talked with him. (Genesis 45:14–15)*

When I was a child, we used to sing an old hymn of faith whose words mirror Joseph's reunion with Benjamin. I'll never forget the joy in that little country church as everyone, from the seasoned saints to the small children, belted out this matchless chorus.

> *"When we all get to heaven, what a day of rejoicing that will be!*
> *When we all see Jesus, we'll sing and shout the victory!"*[24]

⧗ *What hymn of the faith is meaningful to you?*

Craig and I raised five wonderful children and taught each one about Jesus from the day of their long-anticipated birth. When they were babies, I often placed their little hands on the Bible and said, "This is God's Word. We love the Bible. We obey the Bible." I sang "Jesus Loves Me" multiple times daily to these precious gifts God had chosen for us to raise. And every night at bedtime, from birth until the day each left for university, I prayed this prayer over all five children, inserting each name in succession.

> *"Jesus, thank You for _____. Give them happy dreams and happy sleep. Keep them safe and healthy and strong so they can grow up to serve you all the days of their life. And always let them know how much their mom and dad and siblings love them. In Jesus' name I pray. Amen."*

Joseph's reconciliation with his family should give all of us great hope—especially those mothers who have experienced estrangement from their children. As our children grow, they make their own choices, and often those choices do not mirror their Christian upbringing. The story of Joseph is meant to deliver the unmatched expectation that family restoration is part of your future. These jubilant verses are a prophetic picture for anyone whose family has been torn apart by sin and misunderstanding. Eventually, God will write the end of each one of our stories. Never doubt it.

We, as women of the twenty-first century, serve the God of Joseph. We have been instructed by his resolute stand in faith to live an honorable life and to allow God to use us in the middle of our heartache. We will acknowledge His presence daily and then stand back and watch in amazement as God shows us what only He can do.

⧖   *How can you acknowledge the presence of the Lord in your life?*

⧖   *What does it mean for you "to acknowledge the presence of the Lord"?*

⧖   *Why is it important to serve the Lord even when you have a broken heart?*

The Shout of Pharaoh

Pharaoh, the most powerful man in the ancient world, had developed the utmost respect for this little country boy from the insignificant land of Canaan. Joseph, from the very first day he entered the throne room of the king, had not disappointed Pharaoh. Instead, he proved he was, indeed, filled with the Spirit of the Most High God.

> *Now when the news was heard in Pharaoh's house that Joseph's brothers had come, it pleased Pharaoh and his servants. Then Pharaoh said to Joseph, "Say to your brothers, 'Do this: load your beasts and go to the land of Canaan, and take your father and your households and come to me, and I will give you the best of the land of Egypt and you will eat the fat of the land.' Now you are ordered, 'Do this: take wagons from the land of Egypt for your little ones and for your wives, and bring your father and come. Do not concern yourselves with your goods, for the best of all the land of Egypt is yours.' "*
> **(Genesis 45:16–20)**

Pharaoh treated Joseph's family as his very own. Joseph's lifestyle of honor and morality left a legacy that would benefit his children's children. When we make the hard decision to honor the Lord with our emotions and daily choices, it is not merely so we will live a life of favor. It is knowing the favor transcends our own lives and will land in the laps of even our great grandchildren.

Once again, we are reminded that how we act, speak, and emote during the meanwhile seasons of life are of vital importance to the plans and purposes of the Father. Joseph deserved to be mean and angry in prison, but he chose to encourage those around him. Joseph deserved to grow bitter due to extreme mistreatment, but he chose to serve others with an unselfish heart instead.

The Journey of Life

> *Then the sons of Israel did so; and Joseph gave them wagons according to the command of Pharaoh, and gave them provisions for the journey. To each of them he gave changes of garments, but to Benjamin he gave three hundred pieces of silver and five changes of garments. To his father he sent as follows: ten donkeys loaded with the best things of Egypt, and ten female donkeys loaded with grain and bread and sustenance for his father on the journey.*
>
> *So he sent his brothers away, and as they departed, he said to them, "Do not quarrel on the journey." (Genesis 45:21–24)*

Isn't it interesting that Joseph's parting words to his brothers were, "Do not quarrel on the journey"? This is a provocative and intimate piece of conversation we have been made privy to as Joseph's brothers load up for their trek to Canaan to fetch their father. I believe Joseph didn't want his brothers to revert to old, competitive habits once they left the influence of his presence. Joseph yearned for his brothers to leave the past in the past just as he had done. Joseph was hopeful his brothers would latch on to a new life of sweet fellowship as they walked into their future as biological brothers, but also as friends.

⧖   *Do you have an old habit that keeps rearing its ugly head on your journey of life? What is it? Name it.*

⧖   *Now—be done with it!*

I am praying that even as you read this chapter, the Holy Spirit is speaking to you and encouraging you not to bring old sin patterns into the fruitful life God has for you. Perhaps the Holy Spirit is saying to you:

⧗ *Do not worry on your journey.*

⧗ *Do not blame others on your journey.*

⧗ *Do not gossip on your journey.*

⧗ *Do not be afraid on your journey.*

⧗ *What a delight it is to hide God's Word in our hearts. I pray you will take the time to "treasure" our treasure verse today.*

Jesus said, "Blessed are the poor in spirit"—contrary to what we would expect,
brokenness is the pathway to blessing! There are no alternate routes; there are no shortcuts.
The very thing we dread and are tempted to resist is actually
the means to God's greatest blessings in our lives.

—Nancy Leigh DeMoss Wolgemuth
Broken, Surrender, Holiness

Day 4

Here Comes the Future

Can you imagine the shock Jacob experienced when eleven of his sons arrived home? Perhaps he saw them from a distance and had prepared a welcome home dinner for them. Maybe Jacob was waiting on the front porch of the family estate to hear all about their excursion. When his overjoyed sons informed Jacob of the life Joseph now lived, he must have expressed incredulity and even disbelief.

> *Then they went up from Egypt, and came to the land of Canaan to their father Jacob. They told him, saying, "Joseph is still alive, and indeed he is ruler over all the land of Egypt." But he was stunned, for he did not believe them. When they told him all the words of Joseph that he had spoken to them, and when he saw the wagons that Joseph had sent to carry him, the spirit of their father Jacob revived. Then Israel said, "It is enough; my son Joseph is still alive. I will go and see him before I die."*
> **(Genesis 45:25–28)**

After the initial surprising revelation sank into the soul of Jacob and he saw all Joseph had sent to him, he knew what his grown sons had told him was true. The Bible recounts that "the spirit of their father Jacob revived." Suddenly, life returned to his elderly body again. Instantly he was ready and raring to go. This man who had been ravaged by time and sorrow became vibrantly alert and enthusiastically energized.

I can almost hear Jacob saying to his sons, "What are you waiting for? Pack your bags, your wives, and your children. We are going on a family trip. And I refuse to die until I see my son Joseph!"

After the amazing news that Joseph was alive and in a position to take care of his family, Jacob was ready to walk into his future. He couldn't wait to build a new life stirred with hope and all twelve of his sons by his side.

There are times when the meanwhiles of life rob you of your ability to move ahead and hope again. As I read the narrative of the promise born anew in the heart of Jacob, I imagine he declared with a twinkle in his aged eyes, "Let's get on with living."

If Jacob can shake off discouragement and dare to hope again, so can you. Stand up, take out your cane if necessary, and limp into the future. Soon, your limp will become a confident walk and your walk will become an enthusiastic sprint.

⧗   *Good news revolutionized the heart of Jacob. Can you give someone some good news today?*

⧗   *What is one thing in life you are enthusiastically looking ahead to?*

A New Main Character

Jacob now becomes the main character in most of the remaining chapters of Genesis. The Holy Spirit spotlights Jacob, or Israel, almost exclusively from this point until the last few verses of this very first book in the Bible. Because of this focus shift, we will just linger over a few verses, enabling us to glean wisdom and insights about Jacob as we draw this Bible study to a dynamic conclusion.

> *So Israel set out with all that he had, and came to Beersheba, and offered sacrifices to the God of his father Isaac.* **(Genesis 46:1)**

After Jacob's new lease on life was set into motion, his very first action was to worship the Lord. What a marvelous reminder that all the days of our lives should be wrapped up in worship. Regardless of where you are in your meanwhile, take some time to rest from the busyness and worship the Lord. If you are in a transition in life, worship the Lord. If you are limping along, worship the Lord. If you have more of life behind you than in front of you, worship the Lord. If you are at the crossroads of yesterday and tomorrow, worship the Lord.

Are We There Yet?

The journey this highly excited family undertook was just about two hundred miles long. I suppose they couldn't wait to arrive in Egypt knowing Joseph would be there to greet them. Jacob sent Judah on ahead so Joseph would know the date and time of their arrival.

> *All the persons of the house of Jacob, who came to Egypt, were seventy.* **(Genesis 46:27)**

Joseph was so excited he couldn't wait in Egypt for their arrival but went ahead to meet them in the land of Goshen.

> *Now he sent Judah before him to Joseph, to point out the way before him to Goshen; and they came into the land of Goshen. Joseph prepared his chariot and went up to Goshen to meet his father Israel; as soon as he appeared before him, he fell on his neck and wept on his neck a long time. Then Israel said to Joseph, "Now let me die, since I have seen your face, that you are still alive."* **(Genesis 46:28–30)**

Their shared joy must have been enormous and uncontainable. If I were an artist, this is one of the Bible scenes I would love to bring to life on canvas. I can just picture the elderly gentleman, climbing down from his wagon, lifting up his tunic, and walk-running to the son whom he thought was dead. He may have hurried with a limp common to the aged but make no mistake about it—Jacob ran.

And Joseph. As he saw the caravan drawing closer, he likely jumped out of his royal chariot and sprinted toward his father. Joseph was in the arms of his father. Has there ever been a reunion so exuberant and fulfilling? The father and the son were together once again.

This scene paints a picture of our reunion with our Heavenly Father. As we sprint across the finish line of time and enter the glory of eternity . . . Dad will be waiting. He will open His arms wide and into them we will run.

Jacob's life was now complete—he had found Joseph. They were together face to face.

The Blessing

Jacob was a man who knew the power of bestowing a blessing upon others. He was neither envious nor intimidated by the presence of Pharaoh. He blessed everyone with whom he came in contact.

> **Then Joseph brought his father Jacob and presented him to Pharaoh; and Jacob blessed Pharaoh. (Genesis 47:7)**
> **And Jacob blessed Pharaoh, and went out from his presence. (Genesis 47:10)**

Jacob worshipped the Lord and he blessed people—it was his resolute manner of responding to life. We, too, are called to worship God and bless people. It is who we are to our very core. God's will for your life is to worship Him only and to bless the people with whom you come in contact.

⏳ *What does it mean to "bless people"?*

Now Israel lived in the land of Egypt, in Goshen, and they acquired property in it and were fruitful and became very numerous. Jacob lived in the land of Egypt seventeen years; so the length of Jacob's life was one hundred and forty-seven years. (Genesis 47:27–28)

Jacob ended his life better than he started it. He began as a deceiver, but he ended a worshipper. Jacob's story provides a visible demonstration of the promise found in the prophetic book of Haggai.

"The latter glory of this house will be greater than the former,"
says the Lord of hosts, "and in this place I will give peace,"
declares the Lord of hosts.

—Haggai 2:9

The book of Haggai had not yet been written when Jacob was alive, but the same Holy Spirit who inspired the words in the book of Haggai was also the Holy Spirit of Jacob. God's promises are meant for all of eternity, not just for one season of time.

⧗   *What promise in the Bible means the most to you?*

The end of a matter is better than its beginning.

—Ecclesiastes 7:8

From Jacob's history, we can be assured that it is not how we start in life that matters but how we end our days on earth. If you can allow your pain and meanwhiles to develop into the heart of a worshipper and the stance of one who blesses others, you will have lived a grand life, indeed.

⧗   *What is one thing you hope God does for you before you cross your finish line?*

⧗   *What is one thing you hope to do for God before you cross your finish line?*

⧗   *Share your treasure verse with someone today.*

Of one thing I am perfectly sure: God's story never ends with "ashes."

—Elisabeth Elliot
Made for the Journey

Day 5

Greater than Good

Joseph's life would not be complete without honoring his father, Jacob, also known as Israel. We discovered yesterday that the final chapters of the book of Genesis are really a tribute to Joseph's father. Such is the story of each one of us. Our life stories do not stand on their own but we are products of all who came before us—we will leave a legacy for generations yet to come.

⧗ *How are you a product of those people in your heritage who came before you? List one or two people in your family tree who are older than you are and what they contributed to your life.*

⧗ *What legacy do you want to leave for those who come after you?*

His Dying Breath

Perhaps you are unfamiliar with the story of Jacob, Joseph's father, but one of the memorable moments of his young life was the night he wrestled with a man who many believe to be the Lord Himself (Genesis 32). And now, during the closing hours of Jacob's extraordinary life, he no longer wrestled but worshipped.

> **When the time for Israel to die drew near, he called his son Joseph and said to him, "Please, if I have found favor in your sight, place now your hand under my thigh and deal with me in kindness and faithfulness. Please do not bury me in Egypt,**

> *but when I lie down with my fathers, you shall carry me out of Egypt and bury me*
> *in their burial place." And he said, "I will do as you have said." He said, "Swear*
> *to me." So he swore to him. Then Israel bowed in worship at the head of the bed.*
> (Genesis 47:29–31)

Jacob worshipped the Lord with his dying breath. He would not be remembered as the deceiver or wrestler. His legacy for generations to come would be one of genuine worship. The strands of his life harmonized in a powerful symphony of praise to the Lord whom he served.

> *Now it came about after these things that Joseph was told, "Behold, your father is*
> *sick." So he took his two sons Manasseh and Ephraim with him. When it was told to*
> *Jacob, "Behold, your son Joseph has come to you," Israel collected his strength and*
> *sat up in the bed.* (Genesis 48:1–2)

I just love Jacob's resolve to enthusiastically live every single moment given to him. Jacob collected his waning strength so he could spend a few last minutes with Joseph and his two sons. My friend, don't die before you take your dying breath. Strengthen yourself in the Lord and walk fully engaged in the life God has given you. I have often said I am determined to cross my finish line sweaty not rusty.

> *When Israel saw Joseph's sons, he said, "Who are these?" Joseph said to his father,*
> *"They are my sons, whom God has given me here." So he said, "Bring them to me,*
> *please, that I may bless them."* (Genesis 48:8–9)

Jacob spent the final minutes of his life speaking a benediction over the next generation. He refused to die a bitter old man or even a disheartened one, but instead, lavished encouragement and prophetic blessing.

I started the sweet discipline of writing notes to all my grandchildren. I pen one a week and put it in the mail–even for those who live close to me. At this point, I have nine grandchildren, so they each receive an encouraging word and a scripture from Marmee about once every other month. I am determined to be a lavish encourager, so my voice will echo through the hallways of the hearts of my grandchildren after my time on earth is done.

⧗   *If you are a mother or grandmother, what can you do to bless the generations to come?*

⧗ *If you are not a mother, you can still have an impact on the generations to come.*
How could you do that?

> **He blessed Joseph, and said,**
> **"The God before whom my fathers Abraham and Isaac walked,**
> **The God who has been my shepherd all my life to this day,**
>
> **The angel who has redeemed me from all evil,**
> **Bless the lads;**
> **And may my name live on in them,**
> **And the names of my fathers Abraham and Isaac;**
> **And may they grow into a multitude in the midst of the earth."**
> **(Genesis 48:15–16)**

Jacob barely had time to die, he was so intent on blessing the sons and grandsons God had given him. As I grow older, I have determined not to become crotchety, grumpy, or negative. I will provide a glorious demonstration of the goodness of God in one woman's life. I will bless my family despite my feelings and in spite of my age.

Although Jacob could no longer see or hear, he still spoke, and every word that came out of his toothless mouth was a word of grace over each one of his sons (Genesis 49). Jacob likely gasped for air by this point, and yet he still delivered a blessing and a charge.

> **All these are the twelve tribes of Israel, and this is what their father said to them**
> **when he blessed them. He blessed them, every one with the blessing appropriate**
> **to him. Then he charged them and said to them, "I am about to be gathered to my**
> **people . . ." (Genesis 49:28–29)**

What a glorious picture the Holy Spirit has given us of how a saint should go home to the Father. Jacob blessed each of his sons and told them he was about to join the ranks of those who had gone before him and yet he "charged" them. The word *charge* is the Hebrew word *sava* and it means to appoint or "to lay charge upon."[25] Jacob was encouraging his sons, "Go for it. Do it. It's your turn now. This is your moment to live."

> **When Jacob finished charging his sons, he drew his feet into the bed and breathed**
> **his last, and was gathered to his people. (Genesis 49:33)**

⧗   *Whom do you know personally that has left a godly legacy for their family?*

Do You Believe?

After the sons of Jacob buried him, they held a family meeting without Joseph's presence. Fear seized the older sons of Jacob and they felt sure that Joseph would no longer bless them or take care of them.

> *After he had buried his father, Joseph returned to Egypt, he and his brothers, and all who had gone up with him to bury his father.*
>
> *When Joseph's brothers saw that their father was dead, they said, "What if Joseph bears a grudge against us and pays us back in full for all the wrong which we did to him!" So they sent a message to Joseph, saying, "Your father charged before he died, saying, 'Thus you shall say to Joseph, "Please forgive, I beg you, the transgression of your brothers and their sin, for they did you wrong."' And now, please forgive the transgression of the servants of the God of your father." And Joseph wept when they spoke to him. Then his brothers also came and fell down before him and said, "Behold, we are your servants." (Genesis 50:14–18)*

Fear always causes us to act in a manner inappropriate for a child of God. Fear had grabbed hold of the hearts of Joseph's ten older brothers, and they convinced themselves that since Jacob had died, Joseph might be a fake. They thought he would now seek revenge on their lives. When they sent a message that smacked of fear to Joseph, reminding him of their transgressions, Joseph broke down and wept. He sobbed uncontrollably when he realized his brothers were afraid of him.

> *But Joseph said to them, "Do not be afraid, for am I in God's place?" (Genesis 50:19)*

Joseph reminded his insecure, grieving brothers that God was still on the throne. I believe this is an appropriate and incontestable reminder for you and me today.

When you are dealing with human fear—remind yourself that God is still on the throne.

When you are in the throes of grief—remind yourself that God has not abdicated His authority to anyone else.

Tell yourself what Joseph kindly told his brothers, "Don't be afraid. No one is able to take God's place."

⧖   *What are you truly afraid of?*

⧖   *What does God want you to do with this fear?*

There stood Joseph's hulking, middle-aged brothers; some were now balding while others likely had long, gray beards. They had fear, guilt, and unresolved heart hurts in common. However, their main impediment was the refusal to acknowledge the power and goodness of God. Joseph is about to settle that issue at last for these men who had allowed personal disappointment to define God for them.

> *"As for you, you meant evil against me, but God meant it for good in order to bring about this present result, to preserve many people alive. So therefore, do not be afraid; I will provide for you and your little ones." So he comforted them and spoke kindly to them.* **(Genesis 50:20–21)**

Do you believe God will do for you what He did for Joseph? Do you now know the Father is able to take every bad event in your meanwhile and use it for a greater good? Do you believe?

Joseph never would have saved a nation from starvation had he not been trapped in a meanwhile. The "good" God extracts from a sordid evil is far greater than that which a peaceful, uneventful life could ever create. Joseph comforted his desperate brothers and spoke kindly to them. May I share a wonderful piece of information with you?

Jesus, your Brother, wants to comfort you today. He is speaking kindly to you, reminding you of His presence and His partnership with the Father. He is taking your meanwhile—whatever it is—and touching it with His power. Your meanwhile is becoming a miracle!

The most incredible thing about miracles
is that they happen.

—*G. K. Chesterton*
The Blue Cross

THE JOSEPH PRINCIPLE

The Most Important Person

The final and most important person in our line of Joseph-like, God-fearing, uncompromising examples is YOU! The baton is passed and now lies in your hands. Will you receive it with joy? Will you resolve to live every one of your remaining days as a woman who refused to be identified by her circumstances or pain, but by the God whom she serves?

My prayer for you, as we close this final chapter on the stunning life of Joseph, is that you will move forward resolutely. I pray His presence will be your strength through both pain and celebration.

When your heart has been broken by ill-treatment or gargantuan discouragement, I pray you will snuggle up into the presence of the Lord.

I pray you will run from sin and choose to live honorably, all the days of your life.

I pray the name of the Lord will gloriously fill every conversation into which you enter.

I pray you will bless those who have been unkind and that you will minister to those who have been cruel.

I pray you will hear the voice of the Lord and share His wisdom with those around you.

I pray you will store up all the components of an abundant life and generously give it to a world marked by spiritual famine.

I pray you will say to the Lord, "Use me. Fill me. Sustain me. Guide me. Let the breath of God breathe upon my soul!"

I pray you will be more aware of the goodness of God than you are of searing human disappointments.

I pray you will live all your days strengthened by His power and blessing those around you.

Let it be said of you, "God wrote the end of her story, and it was glorious!"

The glory of God is man fully alive!

—St. Irenaeus of Lyons
Against Heresies, ca. AD 180

NOTES

1. Dr. Henry Morris, *So Noted! Genesis Commentary by Dr. Henry Morris* (Green Forest, AR: Masters Books, 2017), 108.

2. Victor P. Hamilton, *The Book of Genesis: Chapters 18-50*, The New International Commentary on the Old Testament (Grand Rapids: William B. Eerdmans, 1995), 406.

3. Kenneth A. Mathews, Genesis 11:27–50:26: An Exegetical and Theological Exposition of Holy Scripture, The New American Commentary, vol. 1B (Nashville: Broadman & Holman, 2005), 669.

4. Hamilton, *Book of Genesis*, 412.

5. Hamilton, *Book of Genesis*, 417.

6. James Montgomery Boice, *Living by Faith: Genesis 37-50*, Genesis: An Expositional Commentary, vol. 3 (Grand Rapids: Baker Books, 1998), 874.

7. Gordon Dunn, "The Martyrdom of John and Betty Stam," OMF, https://omf.org/us/the-martyrdom-of-john-and-betty-stam/.

8. Daniel L. Akin, *Ten Who Changed the World* (Nashville: B&H Publishing, 2012), 158–59.

9. Brad Strait, "A Miracle Inside the Aurora Shooting: One Victim's Story," Celtic Straits, July 23, 2016, https://bradstrait.com/2016/07/23/a-miracle-inside-the-the-aurora-shooting-one-victims-story/.

10. Brad Strait, "Petra Anderson Miracle Updates," Celtic Straits, August 31, 2013, https://bradstrait.com/2013/08/31/petra-anderson-miracle-updates/.

11. Corrie ten Boom said these sentiments everywhere she went and in different ways.

12. Boice, *Living by Faith*, 887.

13. Elisabeth Elliot, *Seeking God's Guidance: A Guided Journey for Discovering God's Will for Your Life* (Grand Rapids: Baker, 2021).

14. Boice, *Living by Faith*, 889.

15. Boice, *Living by Faith*, 890.

16. Morris, *So Noted!*, 115.

17. Boice, *Living by Faith*, 974.

18. Boice, *Living by Faith*, 880.

19. Elisabeth Elliot, *Suffering Is Never for Nothing* (Nashville: B&H Publishing, 2019).

20. Elisabeth Elliot, *Keep a Quiet Heart* (Grand Rapids: Revell, 2008), 20.

21. Ellen Vaughn, *Becoming Elisabeth Elliot* (Nashville: B&H Publishing, 2020), 13.

22. Vaughn, *Becoming Elisabeth Elliot*, 259.

23. Boice, *Living by Faith*, 1043.

24. E. E. Hewitt, "When We All Get to Heaven," 1898.

25. Blue Letter Bible, s.v. "sava," https://www.blueletterbible.org/lexicon/h6680/kjv/wlc/0-1/.